Reading to Belong

Reading to Belong

Identity, Perspective, and Advocacy in the Elementary Grades

Alyson Lamont, Pamela Washington, and Emilie Hard

ROWMAN & LITTLEFIELD
Lanham • Boulder • New York • London

Published by Rowman & Littlefield
An imprint of The Rowman & Littlefield Publishing Group, Inc.
4501 Forbes Boulevard, Suite 200, Lanham, Maryland 20706
www.rowman.com

86-90 Paul Street, London EC2A 4NE

British Library Cataloguing in Publication Information Available

Library of Congress Cataloging-in-Publication Data
Names: Lamont, Alyson, author. | Washington, Pamela, author. | Hard, Emilie, author.
Title: Reading to belong : identity, perspective, and advocacy in the elementary grades / Alyson Lamont, Pamela Washington, and Emilie Hard.
Description: Lanham, Maryland : Rowman & Littlefield, [2024] | Includes bibliographical references.
Identifiers: LCCN 2023056679 (print) | LCCN 2023056680 (ebook) | ISBN 9781475874327 (cloth) | ISBN 9781475874334 (paperback) | ISBN 9781475874341 (ebook)
Subjects: LCSH: Reading (Elementary)—Social aspects. | Belonging (Social psychology) | Social justice and education.
Classification: LCC LB1573 .R76 2024 (print) | LCC LB1573 (ebook) | DDC 372.4—dc23/eng/20231218
LC record available at https://lccn.loc.gov/2023056679
LC ebook record available at https://lccn.loc.gov/2023056680

∞™ The paper used in this publication meets the minimum requirements of American National Standard for Information Sciences—Permanence of Paper for Printed Library Materials, ANSI/NISO Z39.48-1992.

For Everett and Kenneth

Contents

Foreword

I grew up learning to read through a series of books called Dick and Jane. Each book was a colorful collection of stories primarily focused on a boy named Dick, a girl named Jane, and their ever-present dog Spot. There may have been a cat too. I was taught as a little girl to have "fun with Dick and Jane." I saw Dick run, Spot jump, and Jane skip. But what I didn't see during my early years of development were myself, family, or friends as a part of the "American dream." As I was improving my reading skills, I was learning that the sun always shines on this blond-haired, blue-eyed happy-go-lucky two-parent family created by educators William Gray and Zerna Sharp. In 1965, the year I was born, the authors included a Black family who moved into the neighborhood. However, it wasn't until I did some research for this foreword that they existed in my mind. And even still, I can't recall anything about them as a child. In 1954, the *Brown v. Board of Education of Topeka* case made history when the Supreme Court ruled that it was unconstitutional to segregate children based on race. Psychologists Mamie and Kenneth Clark's well-known "doll study" was pivotal in demonstrating that school segregation led to Black children internalizing oppression and therefore a sense of inferiority. Though our schools had been desegregated by this landmark decision, our curriculum still bolstered a Euro-centric monocultural narrative.

While I was learning to read with Dick and Jane, social psychologist William Cross was building on the success of the Clark "doll study" and furthering the work of other Black psychologists. Cross examined Black racial identity development, which he initially referred to as the nigrescence model, revealing the long-term effects of racism once children become adults. It was on my way to becoming a psychologist, during my first year of graduate school, that I encountered Cross's model. Quite frankly it was life changing. There was something about seeing a "model" and recognizing myself in many of its five stages that led me on a journey toward wholeness. Knowing that I was not the only one encumbered by racism somehow eased the pain of what I had internalized and lessened the shame of the ways I had colluded with racism. Cross's work served as a mirror for where I was and a window to where I wanted to be, ultimately setting me on an arduous course of deconstructing feelings I had about myself and the behaviors that follow a lifetime of internalizing inferiority. The residues of racism from my childhood, compounded by daily encounters of anti-Blackness, has required a vigilance on my part to constantly extricate prejudicial messaging, and it has been fatiguing.

The Civil Rights Act may have ended laws that prohibited discrimination and public segregation, but racism is still alive and well. And while Dick and Jane books have long been gone from classroom shelves, culturally relevant literature that provides diverse perspectives and experiences are currently being banned in some school districts. Children of color are still being messaged overtly and covertly that they are an inferior race, solely due to the color of their skin.

Today, psychologists, sociologists, and educators continue to build on the groundwork that was formed not just by Mamie and Kenneth Clark and William Cross but many others, too numerous to name. Thanks to the abundance of research on racial and ethnic identity development, educators are now understanding the important role a multicultural curriculum has in shaping a healthy positive racial identity in early childhood. Lamont, Washington, and Hard have joined forces, bringing together their collective knowledge and experiences. They skillfully equip K–5 educators with tools, strategies, and examples on ways to change the detrimental narratives that have permeated our classrooms for generations. They show teachers how to support their students' development in a way that can lead to healthy outcomes. Children learn the power of their own voices, see themselves as change agents, internalize their beauty and brilliance, and become curious about others. They not only encourage their colleagues to become leaders of this process, they also provide guidance on how to do so with an equity lens.

As I read *Reading to Belong: Identity, Perspective, and Advocacy in the Elementary Grades*, I couldn't help but imagine myself as a little girl in those classrooms. What would it have been like for me as a shy little girl to learn about Ruby Bridges, not as someone just from the past or different from me. But to learn about her story and her struggle and see myself as being like her—someone whose actions could build bridges too? Maybe I wouldn't have had to wait until graduate school to find the power in my voice if I partook in the read-aloud *My Voice Is a Trumpet* and unpacked its message with my teacher and peers. I can imagine myself taking pride in speaking up when other kids were bullied rather than being content with the passive role of "at least" not being the bully. What if during my formative years rather than watching Dick and Jane jump rope, teachers were using books as mirrors and windows to equip me with the language and tools to understand my own experiences and other people's too. *Reading to Belong* equips teachers to expand students' language and understanding of social justice issues. The authors highlight throughout how this can lead to a sense of belonging for students, key to forming a healthy racial identity no matter their race. Any educator trying out the strategies outlined in this book will also gain the benefit of learning while teaching. Lamont, Washington, and Hard are no strangers to the fears and challenges that come with doing racial justice work. Any fears teachers may have about making mistakes are lessened through the authors' guidance. The risk educators are willing to take to incorporate their students' lives in the curriculum and build them up as change makers will benefit them and our society for years to come.

Lamont, Washington, and Hard understand that children should not have to wait until they become adults to unravel the insidious racial messages portrayed about them and others. They know that racism won't end today, or tomorrow, or for many years to come and therefore see the urgency in helping our children to decipher it now. These three educators show other educators a way to teach their students how to interrogate past and present damaging narratives, so they are empowered to take part in creating something new, something different from what our country has ever known. It is what and how we teach our children that will mitigate the impacts of racism and alleviate a lifetime of wrestling with unhealthy messages about themselves and others.

Reading to Belong: Identity, Perspective, and Advocacy in the Elementary Grades is a necessary read for any elementary teacher, school, or district committed to racial justice. It shifts the check-the-box approach, confronts the "I don't know what to do" comments, to "Here's a place to begin." It recognizes that educators are essential in shaping a child's sense of belonging and that, when equipped with the right books, that child can disrupt the dangerous single story. The authors graciously invite their colleagues to lean in and support the forming of their students' racial identities, knowing that educators will find themselves rewarded with socially just classrooms and learning communities.

—Caprice D. Hollins, PsyD, is cofounder of Cultures Connecting, providing keynotes, workshops, and consulting on race relations. She is the author of *Inside Out: The Equity Leader's Guide to Undoing Institutional Racism* and coauthor of *Diversity, Equity, and Inclusion: Strategies for Facilitating Conversations on Race.* She is a Seattle 2020 TEDx speaker on "What White People Can Do to Move Race Conversations Forward."

Preface

When we started writing this book, waves of states had begun pushing back on critical race theory (CRT). As of 2021, five states have banned CRT in schools, with many others introducing similar legislation.[1] Often without a nuanced understanding of what CRT entails, many communities are crafting forceful campaigns to ensure that discussions around race do not occur in our nation's classrooms. While this book does not specifically take up a CRT lens, we do argue that conversations around race—and other identity markers—merit space in even our earliest classrooms.

We see urgency in this work amid political turmoil, which is compounded by the ongoing trauma from a global pandemic. Systemic discrimination in our schools, economy, and political systems are barriers for many children and can no longer be ignored. Furthermore, we argue that children who face little to no systemic barriers in education are positioned to work toward a better world for all, one where all children belong and have opportunities to succeed. Having conversations about race and belonging are imperative for everyone to be engaged in.

This book is designed for K–5 educators—specifically teachers, instructional coaches, curriculum specialists, paraeducators, and school and district administrators. This book will share snapshots of conversations happening in real classrooms that center around identity, perspective, and action. We highlight conversations that equip students with language to understand their identity and the identities of others, while developing a sense of agency to work toward a more just world. In particular, this text will seek to answer these questions:

- How might an understanding of mirrors and windows help students gain an understanding of themselves and empathy for the experiences of others?
- How can teachers enter into discussions with students about identity, understanding, and advocacy?
- How can educational leaders employ an equity lens to effect change and support a sense of belonging for all students?

CONTEXT FOR THIS WORK

The setting for our specific work occurs across several neighboring school districts located in the Pacific Northwest. While these districts overlap in some ways, they diverge in both the populations they serve as well as their pathways to promote equity within their systems.

All three districts are increasingly diverse, and are considered high-performing districts.

The first district has a diverse population of approximately 15,300 students in pre-K through twelfth grade at four high schools, four middle schools, fifteen elementary schools, and an early childhood learning center. Student enrollment in 2022–2023 was 21 percent White, 25 percent Asian, 28 percent Latinx, 15 percent Black, and 10 percent two or more races. Low income percentage was 54 percent.

The school system strives to remove barriers and work toward outcomes that enable all students to realize their potential and maximize opportunities. A formal Diversity, Equity and Inclusion (DEI) Committee was established to empower critical conversations about equity and lead to action steps. The DEI Committee currently has three areas of focus: communicating and amplifying equity efforts throughout the district community, monitoring and supporting the implementation of DEI online learning modules for district employees, and developing a vision of culturally relevant and responsive practices in partnership with the Department of Curriculum, Instruction, and Assessment.

Enrollment demographics in 2022–2023 for the second district indicated 62 percent White, 13 percent Asian, 11 percent Latinx, 3 percent Black, and 10 percent two or more races. Low income percentage was 19 percent. Approximately 9,100 students attend the six elementary schools, two middle schools, and the one high school. For three decades, the district has maintained a focus on critical thinking skills such as problem solving, analysis, synthesis, and evaluation, and on habits of mind such as empathy, inquisitiveness, persistence, and flexibility. These skills provide an important focus beyond academic content, and teachers provide opportunities for students to practice and reflect upon their growth in these skill areas.

In recent years, a system's focus on equity has begun, with the overall goal being to support a welcoming, safe, and inclusive environment for each student and adult in order to promote a sense of belonging for each individual. Multiple long-range goals are articulated in the areas of:

- Improving school climate
- Amplifying student voices
- Increasing diverse family engagement
- Providing professional development for staff
- Using an equity lens for making decisions
- Hiring and retaining a more diverse staff
- Revising curriculum to provide multiple perspectives and relevancy

An inclusion, diversity, and equity policy was approved unanimously by the school board in May 2022. Addressing all of these areas supports a comprehensive approach to building an equitable school system.

The third district has almost twenty thousand students and is a high-performing, suburban school system that is rapidly diversifying. While in the 2006–2007 school year district three's student body was over 73 percent White, the 2022–2023 enrollment demographics reveal less than 50 percent (42 percent) White students, 35 percent Asian students, followed by 10.5 percent Latinx students, 10 percent two or more races, and a small percentage of Black students. The district includes four high schools, six middle schools, and sixteen elementary schools. The low income percentage was 13 percent.

To address enrollment trends and data showing the opportunity gaps among marginalized groups of students, the third district established a formal equity policy in 2018, which focuses on respect, inclusion, and ensuring that all students have opportunities to thrive in school. Framed by cultural competency and culturally relevant pedagogy, the equity policy recognizes that institutional barriers exist within the system, and pledges to work toward the elimination of these barriers while maintaining high academic standards for all students.[2]

The equity policy doesn't operate in isolation, but in partnership with other district initiatives. For example, the Equity Department leads professional development work for administrators, school staff, and the community around culturally relevant practices, focusing on how our individual identities impact relationships with students and one another.

We share the context of these school districts to illustrate the advantages and challenges that exist. In contrast to the diversifying student bodies across all of these neighboring districts, the racial makeup of the teacher and administrative workforce has remained largely unchanged and primarily White in districts two and three, revealing significant

Preface

cultural, racial, and linguistic hurdles. Outside of formal district systems, there are pockets of professionals engaging deeply in equity and inclusion work. For example, professional book clubs serve as informal think tanks that wrestle with anti-racist teaching practices.

While interest from teachers across these school systems—and beyond—is burgeoning, they nonetheless face challenges in deeply integrating this work. Some simply do not see the urgency. For others, fear of resistance from community members, as well as not having the tools to facilitate these conversations with students, stalls efforts. These tensions in our systems reflect a larger world of social and political unrest, where our nation's schools are often caught in the middle.

Therefore, despite these initiatives, conversations around equity and diversity continue to vary widely. The small grassroots efforts are notable; however, there is still much work to be done to ensure that equity is the lens from which a system operates. Often, equity can become a check mark or a bullet point in a long list of considerations (when adopting a new curricular material or policy, for example), rather than a nuanced lens from which every decision is made.

OUR *WHY* AND GOALS FOR THIS BOOK

Knowing our *why* for engaging in this work gives us resilience, strength, and courage to continue striving for educational justice. Ensuring that all students find a sense of belonging in our schools is the right thing to do . . . it is central as we strive for a healthy, inclusive democracy. Teaching students to question what they read, consume, and hear prepares the next generation to wrestle cognitively with social issues, bringing an understanding of their own identity to these discussions. Teachers are on the front lines, and therefore need to be equipped with tools to facilitate critical conversations with students. The purpose of this book is to do just that.

I, Alyson Lamont, was a student who thrived in school. I was a White, middle-class, cisgender, neurotypical female from a family of educators, and school made sense to me; I navigated it with ease. In large part, I achieved academic success because I had an identity that was valued in school. I didn't yet have an awareness of inequality and the ways that I was unknowingly perpetuating it. It was not until my years as an adult researcher in education that I came to understand the many layers of my privilege, and learned how to have critical conversations across lines of difference. I had learned how to be a reader in the classrooms of my childhood, but I hadn't learned to *act*. In our highly politicized and contentious society, it is my belief that we can and should equip children with the skills to create a more just world.

I, Pamela Washington, am a Black cisgender female who is, in the words of Michelle Obama, still on the path of becoming comfortable in my own skin while heightening the awareness of the world I truly live in. I grew up as a middle child in Seattle, and race was never a focus of conversations at the table—this was done as a means to protect us from the harsh realities of the world we lived in and the racist experiences of both parents. This attempt of shielding and protection resulted in growing up with my head in the sand, assimilating to the dominant culture of Whiteness while unknowingly unaware of my identity. In essence, I was completely oblivious to the impacts of systemic racism in my life. At the age of forty-one, after learning I was pregnant with a son, a Black son, life began. While civil unrest was spreading throughout the world, *scales of ignorance* fell from my eyes. What unearthed within me was an unrelenting dedication to the education profession. The hope is that this book is a tool for educators looking to cultivate identity-affirming experiences and learning spaces for all students, especially those historically marginalized.

I, Emilie Hard, am a White, cisgender, middle-class female who has spent more than forty years in education. My roles have included parent, teacher, curriculum specialist, principal, assistant superintendent for teaching and learning, and equity director, and it's been fascinating to view education from many different perspectives. Although I grew up in a family who served as a "Friendship Family" by welcoming international college students into our family and community, it wasn't until about a decade ago that I became aware of the extent of my privilege. I began advocating for equitable practices in my school district and communities, and I believe that it takes all of us to work toward social justice. While my early involvement with international students enabled me to value diversity, it was listening to voices from diverse K–12 students about their lived experiences in our school systems that propelled me to become an advocate. The more I learned, the more I realized there was to learn. I needed to find the courage to make a difference. DEI work is part of my being now, and I will always continue to work toward understanding, inclusion, and equity. One of the ways in which I'm committed to doing that is to support teachers in having courageous conversations with students. In the words of Ibram X. Kendi in *How to Be an Antiracist,* "Courage is not the absence of fear, but the strength to do what is right in the face of it."[3]

Our own identities and experiences as educators both overlap and diverge in significant ways, and this book is a product of our mutual reflections. Throughout this book, we will therefore write as the collective "we" unless otherwise stated. This text represents our ongoing pursuit of equitable opportunities for all students, and is meant to support educators with tools to engage in courageous conversations.

Paulo Freire, often considered to be one of the founders of critical literacy, argues that individuals must be able to both read the *word* and read the *world* in order to advocate for oneself and for those who have experienced oppression.[4] It is not enough for our students to learn to decode if they do not take up language to enact change in the world. Similarly, without the skills needed to navigate printed texts, students will continue to face barriers to social and political engagement, and will be excluded from those conversations. Thus, learning to read occurs while simultaneously learning about the world and one's place in it, rather than as a precursor. This perspective contrasts with the traditional and now largely outdated view that students first learn to read, and then read to learn. As lifelong educators, we argue that even before children are conventionally reading books, they are *reading the world* around them. All students, even our youngest, come to our classroom and school doors with experiences and background knowledge, and they don't wait for conventional reading to begin to make sense of their world. In fact, if we wait until students are conventionally reading to begin having critical conversations, it may be too late.

For those who say that children need to learn to decode with regular phonetic words prior to reading more ethnically diverse words and names, we would point to Freire's position. For example, children are learning underlying messages about the world even as they read math word problems or decodable texts. In the absence of diverse names in these texts, the message that is conveyed may be that names from the dominant social group are the norm. By including names from a variety of cultures and backgrounds in texts and curriculum, the learning material becomes more accessible and relevant to a wider audience of students.

Students learn about the world around them both in the formal curriculum, as well as in the informal and sometimes "hidden curriculum" of schooling.[5] These informal classroom conversations are often where students curate their identities, and learn what really matters both in schools as well as the larger society. For example, author Stephanie Jones describes a classroom setting where many family members of students are incarcerated, yet when students share these experiences, the statements are ignored by teachers.[6] In discussions like these, the lived experiences of students can be accepted as a form of knowledge, or they can be sanctioned.[7] In the instance that Jones describes, students learned from an early age that the values of school clashed with having incarcerated family members, and many students decided to stay silent about this aspect of their life. Too often, this is still the case with students who have backgrounds that differ from school authority figures (who are often White, middle class, cisgender, able bodied, and neurotypical). This book attempts to illustrate concretely how classrooms can become places where all students belong, and confidently tell the stories of who they are.

Using language—whether in information, literature, art, or communication—is how humans transform the world. We take up the ideas from Freire and others, and hope that all children read broadly to understand themselves and their identity, while having empathy for the experiences of others. Furthermore, we hope that children become knowledgeable, empathetic, and passionate citizens who advocate for a more just world. This, in part, begins in our classrooms, in our conversations with students.

Mike Maryanski, a former superintendent and mentor, wisely explained that when implementing any systems change, teachers will need to have answers to these two questions:

- Why is this important?
- Can I do it?

In this book, we will provide guidance on both of these questions through examples and through our own collective insights. Thank you for joining us in this work . . . now, let's go!

NOTES

1. Zalaznik, M. (2021). *2 states, and counting, ban critical race theory in schools.* District Administration. Retrieved from https://districtadministration.com/states-ban-teaching-critical-race-theory-schools/.
Adams, et al. (2021). *Map: See which states have passed critical race theory bills.* NBC News. Retrieved from https://www.nbcnews.com/news/nbcblk/map-see-which-states-have-passed-critical-race-theory-bills-n1271215.

2. Ladson-Billings, G. (1995). Toward a theory of culturally relevant pedagogy. *American Educational Research Journal, 32*(3), 465–491.

3. Kendi, I. X. (2019). *How to be an antiracist.* London: One World.

4. Freire, P. (1970). *Pedagogy of the oppressed.* London: Penguin.

5. Apple, M. W. (1971). The hidden curriculum and the nature of conflict. *Interchange, 2*(4), 27–40.

6. Jones, S. (2006). *Girls, social class, and literacy: What teachers can do to make a difference.* Portsmouth, NH: Heinemann.

7. Esteban-Guitart, M., & Moll, L. C. (2014). Funds of identity: A new concept based on the funds of knowledge approach. *Culture & Psychology, 20*(1), 31–48.

Acknowledgments

First and foremost: to teachers, who make such a lasting impact on the lives of their students, thank you for taking the time to read this book. Thank you for reflecting on your own learning and for being deliberate in creating spaces where *all* students belong. Special thanks to those teachers who invited us into their classrooms to show us how courageous conversations happen: Wendy, Lisa, Tori, Katie, Madyson, Miller, Sara, Stacey, Kristi, Andrea, McKay, and Peggy. Much appreciation to those educators who shared their insights with us during interviews: Tony Davis, Dr. Damien Pattenaude, and teachers Maura, Sylvia, Jordan, Jen, and Dreya. We also want to acknowledge the librarians who are fighting to make sure that diverse books are available to all children. You are so important to this work.

We cannot thank the team at Rowman & Littlefield enough, especially Jasmine Holman, for believing in this project. Thank you for your guidance. Our gratitude also to fellow educator Jessica Fishman for reading and offering feedback on early drafts of this book.

Endless appreciation to our mentor, Dr. Caprice Hollins, for showing us her *why*, for demonstrating the *how*, and for her unending support as we've supported our school districts in becoming more equitable systems that "walk the talk" in supporting safe, inclusive, welcoming places for all students. She has demonstrated the vulnerability, humility, and learning stance that we aspire to as we support invitational approaches to DEI goals. Her coaching has inspired us and supported us in believing that we can all make a difference in the lives of current and future generations to create a more socially just world.

We are so grateful to our friends and families for their support throughout this process. Alyson would like to thank her parents, Jeff and Emilie Hard (yes, *that* Emilie Hard). You've always believed that I could do anything that I set my mind to. To my professors and colleagues from Teachers College: thank you for teaching me to be a writer. Michelle Moon, I'm grateful to have had you as a thought partner during this process. Finally, to my partner, Warren, and son, Everett, you are my everything. Thank you for encouraging me to take the leap.

Pamela would like to first and foremost, thank God from whom all blessings flow. To my husband for his unwavering support and encouragement while pursuing my passions. To my son, Kenneth, whose mere existence fuels my why for this work. And to my CoL Crew for their constant iron-sharpening-iron humble accountability.

Emilie would like to thank her husband, Jeff, for his unwavering support. To my daughter, Alyson, and son, Andrew, for being open minded and respectful of others; I'm incredibly proud of the people you've become. To my mother, thank you for teaching me that there is strength in diversity and that getting to know diverse people from different cultures is a foundation for developing empathy. To Mike Hanson and Ron Thiele, for taking a chance on me to grow as an equity leader.

Introduction: Why This Work?

Human beings are not built in silence, but in word, in work, in action-reflection.—Paulo Freire[1]

As you read this introduction, you'll find it more theoretical than the other chapters, which offer practical applications. Feel free to skim, skip, and jump around as you need.

This book is anchored in critical literacy, as we believe that language, literacy, and texts have the power to reflect our own lived experiences, as well as invite us to empathize with the experiences of others. And as Freire reminds us: to act.[2] Critical literacy is grounded in the belief that literacy is not simply decoding but is also social language—communication (speaking/listening/nonverbal), printed texts, images, artistic expression, and more. Teachers have to make decisions constantly—and one of the biggest decisions is how to spend instructional time. In our discussions with teachers, we learned that it is critical literacy that sometimes seems secondary to the more pressing needs to assess, instruct, and (due to a global pandemic) make up for so-called learning loss. And yet, ensuring that each student has an opportunity to engage in critical literacy is more urgent than ever.

CRITICAL LITERACY: HOW THIS WORK IS FRAMED

Critical literacy argues that the world is a text and that students are agents in making sense of their world, as well as active participants within it. In

1

fact, language is central to how we see and navigate the world, something that is unique to the *Homo sapiens* species.[3] Rooted in language, critical literacy aims to uncover, name, and disrupt dominant narratives that uphold systems of marginalization by giving students access to the tools needed to do so.

In taking up critical literacy, it is crucial to distinguish between critical thinking skills and critical work. Critical thinking skills have often been called noncognitive skills, and refer to competencies such as perseverance, grit, and creativity.[4] While important to educating the whole child, these noncognitive skills are individual attributes. Critical work takes this a step further, and is aimed at channeling these attributes into action for the *collective* good. In education, this means cultivating individual attributes while also creating a community of care and justice. Put simply: each student can contribute to a sense of belonging in our schools while also pursuing individual achievements. One doesn't negate the other. Engagement in critical work means to examine our place within social systems and to move the needle toward justice for all. *In other words, we want students to be able to recognize systems of power, access them, and ultimately shift them to be more inclusive.*

Identity and Critical Literacy

A focus on identity is intimately tied to critical literacy. Students develop their identities in response to the inherent messages that they encounter in their communities, through the media, within popular culture, and of course, within the texts provided to them in school. Each individual has invisible identity markers such as religious beliefs, hobbies, cultural background, socioeconomic status, traumatic experiences, family role, and more. Professor James Paul Gee defines identities as participation in various groups.[5] The way that we dress, which friends we align ourselves with, the modes of transportation that we have access to, and of course, the ways in which we interact with others help to construct our identity in meaningful ways.[6] For example, we might identify as a "voracious reader," a "passionate educator," and a "political activist." These identities are continually formed through our actions and our language, and are related yet distinct from our often more visible identity markers (race, ethnicity, gender, etc.). Our identity kits, both the visible and invisible, are how we present ourselves to the world.[7]

From an early age, students begin reading the world around them, and as they do so, they decide who they want to be in the world. In some instances, identities can be imposed upon individuals, such as how a teacher discusses a student and their perceived ability, or how a caregiver uses stereotypical gendered language and toys with a child. As students learn about their place in school and the world, they are also learning about—and creating—their identities.

Also central to our identity is how others see us. This is why, as educators, the language that we use with students matters greatly. Peter Johnston reminds us that "building an identity means . . . developing a sense of what it feels like to be that sort of person and belong in certain social spaces."[8]

Rather than referring to a student as a *low* reader, for example, we might say, "This student likes to read graphic novels." This not only is asset-based language, but maintains high expectations for students while fostering a positive identity around reading. Furthermore, we want to refrain from labeling students with a single identity. By labeling a student as a special education student, we ignore the multifaceted identity that the child embodies. Referring to the child as someone with unique strengths and needs recognizes the whole person.

What Critical Literacy Is Not

Critical literacy is not a lesson, a unit, or an add-on. Rather, it is a lens that frames the way we approach education and schooling, just as culturally relevant pedagogy or culturally responsive teaching might similarly be applied to this work.[9] We have chosen to frame this work around critical literacy in particular because texts, and conversations anchored around texts, are our chosen focus for this work with young children. Which read-aloud to select for your class, for example, becomes a conscious choice when applying a critical literacy lens. Selecting a *typical* or seemingly *neutral* text is just as much a statement about our beliefs about students and their identities as selecting a text that highlights diversity, equity, or inclusion. For example, reading a text that features mostly White characters to avoid discussions about race may signal to students that particular identities are valued in school over others. Critical literacy draws attention to these deliberate choices and argues that the texts that we choose to pick up and display in our classrooms matter immensely.

A problematic use of critical literacy is choosing to highlight diverse texts during opportune moments—Black History Month or during holidays, for example, which sends a message to students that their experience can be reduced to a cultural unit or as a token of diversity. For this reason, we stress that the classroom snapshots highlighted in this book are not isolated events, but are instead embedded in ongoing conversations around issues of identity and inclusion.

Finally, critical literacy and explorations into identity do not come at the expense of academic rigor, but rather bolster it. While engaging in literacy toward social action, we must also be conscious that we are indeed teaching students the language skills needed to access what Lisa Delpit calls the gatekeeping "codes of power."[10] What this means is that while we want students doing critical work, it's equally important that they gain foundational academic skills. As Delpit argues further, in order to change society, you need to be able to access and participate in it, which is often done so through language. This is precisely Freire's notion of reading the *word*, and the *world*.[11] Rigorous academic work can be pursued alongside a deep understanding of oneself and belonging to a community, rather than separately.

Gholdy Muhammad argues for a historically responsive literacy (HRL) framework that includes the concurrent cultivation of a positive identity, skills, and intellect, as well as a critical lens that can be applied to curricular lessons in any subject area.[12] This framework, in particular, is rooted in the literacy learning of Black communities and, while beneficial for all students, is designed specifically for those who identify as Black and Brown. Our use of critical literacy will examine a wider variety of identity markers (language, culture, and ethnicity to name a few), some of which are prominent in our communities and thus highlighted in this work.

Critical literacy, like many other overlapping frameworks, focuses on a duality of needs—both honoring students for the talented individuals they are and preparing them to succeed in an unequal world.

Young Children and Critical Literacy

Another tenet of critical literacy is the belief that even our youngest learners are capable of engaging in deliberate, meaningful conversations. Children are not blank canvases where teachers deposit knowledge; instead, children come to school as curious thinkers and meaning-makers even before they can conventionally read. Celia Genishi and Anne Haas Dyson remind us that "because children appropriate cultural material from adult-dominated words, it should be no surprise that they, like us, grapple with human relationships, like friendship, love, and battles (metaphoric or otherwise), and with societal structures, like gender and race."[13] In fact, when we do not tap into those voices and questions in our classroom conversations, it doesn't mean that students aren't asking them; rather, students may not feel that school is a safe space for these critical discussions. The example of incarcerated family members that Stephanie Jones describes (referenced in the preface) is a prime example of this.[14] For this reason, the role of educators in nudging students toward empathy, understanding, and advocacy is paramount.

LITERATURE AS AN ACCESS POINT: GETTING STARTED WITH CRITICAL CONVERSATIONS

Teachers taking up critical perspectives in literacy instruction has been gaining traction for some time. This is particularly true for new teachers—those coming out of a university program and those interviewing (in many locations, a commitment to equity is a component of the interview process). Overall, an emphasis on rethinking both our school libraries and our classroom libraries is continuing to grow as critical perspectives become more familiar. Integrating new texts is intended to diversify our collections as a whole, rather than be introduced for single units or as a specific genre of literature.

As Chimamanda Adichie argues in her TED talk "The Danger of a Single Story," the goal is to provide different perspectives so that our understanding is more complete.[15] We want to work against a single narrative of what a group of people might be like, and instead, show complexity and nuance to our students. Practically, this work requires a quality, high-interest, diverse collection of literature to work with. Many educators are conscious of having collections that represent their student populations (we will discuss *mirror* texts at the end of this chapter). School librarians have spearheaded these efforts for years, guided by the framework put forth by the American Association of School Libraries (AASL), which highlights inclusion, inquiry, collaboration, and critical thinking.[16] Suggestions for building a robust classroom library are included in appendix A.

Pause & Reflect: How might you sift through children's literature to find and curate a meaningful collection?

The publishing world of children's literature is responding to the call for these texts, and quality, inclusive literature is being released every day. However, there are more children's literature blogs and suggested book lists than we could possibly count, let alone consult. This can be overwhelming, and educators refer to diverse texts in multiple ways: mirrors and windows, counternarratives, and "own voices." Which language are we choosing to use and why, when it comes to curating diverse collections?

Mirrors and Windows

Rudine Bishop pioneered the concept of children's books operating as mirrors and windows.[17] Bishop conceptualizes some books as mirrors, reflecting back to the reader an image of themselves (e.g., a strong Black girl). Helping students develop positive identities is partly due to the representation in literature that they may or may not see. Representations of specific groups (religious, cultural, linguistic, etc.) assist individual students in finding a sense of belonging within their school.

By contrast, windows offer the reader a glimpse into another perspective or experience. Literature that operates as windows can build bridges for students, developing understanding and empathy across lines of difference. Bishop argues that these understandings, and our ability to solve complex social problems, can begin quite simply with our experiences with literature. We agree.

Importantly, students need mirrors and windows simultaneously. If mirrors are overemphasized, students may center their experience (particularly deleterious for students who belong to the dominant group). For students who have been marginalized, however, mirrors are paramount to cultivating identity and self-worth. Mirrors and windows have been a helpful, pragmatic framework, and this language continues to be used by educators today.

Counternarratives

"Counternarrative" is a widely used term when seeking children's literature that challenges dominant norms and stereotypes. The images and storylines presented in a counternarrative intentionally run "counter" to dominant cultural portrayals.[18]

A quintessential example of a counternarrative is Robert Munsch's *The Paper Bag Princess*, which offers students a counternarrative to a dominant fairy tale: a female princess being saved and ultimately marriage (or "happily ever after").[19] In *The Paper Bag Princess*, however, the princess saves the prince and chooses to remain happily alone.

Other counternarratives are books such as: *Cece Loves Science* and *Eyes That Kiss in the Corners*.[20] These texts have positive narratives about gender expression and family structures, as well as self-affirming portrayals of gender and race (particularly in underrepresented ways, such as females of color in science fields). The power in counternarratives is deliberately contrasting them with a more dominant storyline, and facilitating intentional discussions about these contrasts.[21]

"Own Voices"

Building on concepts of counternarratives, mirrors, and windows, many professionals in the field of children's literature have championed "own voices" in order to prioritize the narratives of those so often left out of publishing. "Own voices" operates as a hashtag on social media platforms (started in 2015 by Corinne Duyvis) and highlights diverse texts written by authors from marginalized groups. This movement has asked publishers and educators to look at the content of children's literature, but also who is writing and illustrating. Moving away from White authors writing books about children of color, and instead highlighting these "own voices" is intended to tell stories from the inside (rather than the outside or the dominant culture), while simultaneously investing in authors who have been marginalized. This brings up very important questions of authorship: *Who gets to write about what (and whom)?*

For many years, this term gained traction but now is being phased out due to its vague nature, as well as the potential for texts to be mislabeled as "own voices" without the intent of diverse representation (for example, books labeled as "own voices" could perpetuate dominant narratives).

Literature is an access point for critical work, and there are many different ways to approach curating an inclusive collection. Whether teachers consider mirrors and windows or seek out counternarratives, intentionally diversifying the literature that we put in the hands of our students is key. For our purposes in this work, we choose to use the language of mirrors and windows to discuss students deepening an understanding of themselves, experiencing different perspectives, and ultimately using this knowledge to change their world for the better.

HOW TO READ THIS BOOK

Chapter 1 will describe how teachers set up their classroom to have these types of discussions: norms, expectations, and values. After all, creating safe spaces is a precursor to diving into more complex discussions. We recommend that you read chapter 1 next.

The chapters that follow do not necessarily need to be read in order, but the themes presented in the chapters do build on one another. Chapters 2 through 4 are grounded in snapshots from real classrooms with teachers who are engaging in this work with students (and have graciously opened their classrooms to us). Chapter 2 will dive into student identity and an understanding of the self, and what it means to locate and use *mirror* texts. Chapter 3 moves into the concept of *window* texts, where students will use texts to gain an understanding of the experiences of others, and thus develop empathy and perspective. Chapter 4 culminates the progression of classroom snapshots with discussions that encourage students to advocate in their communities—to learn that they can make a difference in their own classrooms and communities. In these snapshots, we will use the social justice standards created by the organization Learning for Justice in order to ground our observations.[22] These standards encompass four domains: identity, diversity, justice, and action.

Chapter 5 provides relevant examples of how teachers and staff have navigated unexpected conversations with students and caregivers, and advocated for equity work in their buildings. Chapter 6 encourages readers of this book to be leaders in this work, whether that is with their own students, professional colleagues, or within a school or district. Organized in sections for starting with self and working with others, strategies, approaches, and informal and formal roles are discussed. Finally, suggested book lists for each remaining chapter are provided.

NOTES

1. Freire, P. (1970). *Pedagogy of the oppressed*, p. 69. London: Penguin.

2. Freire, P. (1970). *Pedagogy of the oppressed*. London: Penguin.

3. Harari, Y. (2018). Sapiens: *A brief history of humankind*. Toronto, ON: McClelland & Stewart.

4. Tough, P. (2013). *How children succeed: Grit, curiosity, and the hidden power of character*. Boston: Houghton Mifflin Harcourt; Duckworth, A. (2018). *Grit: The power of passion and perseverance*. New York: Scribner.

5. Gee, J. P. (2005). *An introduction to discourse analysis*. New York: Routledge.

6. Zacher, J. C. (2009). Christina's worlds: Negotiating childhood in the city. *Educational Studies, 45*(3), 262–279.

7. Gee, J. P. (2000). Chapter 3: Identity as an analytic lens for research in education. *Review of Research in Education, 25*(1), 99–125.

8. Johnston, P. (2004). *Choice words*, p. 23. Portland, ME: Stenhouse.

9. Ladson-Billings, G. (2014). Culturally relevant pedagogy 2.0: Aka the remix. *Harvard Educational Review, 84*(1), 74–84.
Hammond, Z. (2014). *Culturally responsive teaching and the brain: Promoting authentic engagement and rigor among culturally and linguistically diverse students.* Thousand Oaks, CA: Corwin.

10. Delpit, L. (2006). *Other people's children: Cultural conflict in the classroom*, p. xxvi. New York: New Press.

11. Freire, P. (1970). *Pedagogy of the oppressed*. London: Penguin.

12. Muhammad, G. (2020). *Cultivating genius: An equity framework for culturally and historically responsive literacy*. New York: Scholastic.

13. Genishi, C., & Dyson, A. H. (2009). *Children, language, and literacy: Diverse learners in diverse times*, p. 105. New York: Teachers College Press.

14. Jones, S. (2006). *Girls, social class, and literacy: What teachers can do to make a difference.* Portsmouth, NH: Heinemann.

15. Adichie, C. (2009). *The danger of a single story* [Video]. TEDGlobal Conferences. Retrieved from https://www.ted.com/talks/chimamanda _ngozi_adichie_the_danger_of_a_single_story/

16. American Association of School Librarians. (2022). *National School Library Standards.* Retrieved from https://standards.aasl.org/framework

17. Bishop, R. S. (1990, March). *Windows and mirrors: Children's books and parallel cultures* [Paper presentation], pp. 3–12. California State University Reading Conference, San Bernardino: 14th Annual Conference.

18. Luttrell, W. (2013). Children's counter-narratives of care: Towards educational justice. *Children & Society, 27*(4), 295–308.

19. Munsch, R. (1980). *The paper bag princess.* Des Moines, IA: Turtleback Books.

20. Derting, K., & Johannes, S. (2020). *Cece loves science.* New York: Greenwillow Books.

Ho, J. (2021). *Eyes that kiss in the corners.* New York: HarperCollins.

21. Bamberg, M., & Andrews, M. (2004). *Considering counter narratives: Narrating, resisting, making sense.* Amsterdam: John Benjamins.

22. Southern Poverty Law Center (2021). *Frameworks.* Learning for Justice. Retrieved from https://www.learningforjustice.org/frameworks

1

✝

Classroom Communities
Foundations for Safe Conversation Spaces

Fitting in is about assessing a situation and becoming who you need to be in order to be accepted. Belonging, on the other hand, doesn't require us to change who we are; it requires us to be who we are.—Brené Brown[1]

Before embarking on critical conversations with students, it is essential that teachers create a classroom culture that is conducive to community, inquiry, and empathy. Students need to trust that their classroom and school environments are spaces where they will be accepted in order to share aspects of their identity.

Grounded in the work of scholars such as Paulo Freire, Lisa Delpit, and Zaretta Hammond, we lean on our critical literacy framework to build foundations that will allow for the conversations that teachers are eager to have. Considering both the physical space of a classroom as well as the ethos of the classroom is important, and this chapter offers insights in how teachers can collaboratively construct safe conversation spaces.

SETTING UP YOUR PHYSICAL SPACE

As we've learned from Paulo Freire, students learn to read the *word* and the *world* in tandem, and our classrooms are no different.[2] As students take in the physical space of a classroom, they are simultaneously reading the values of the classroom. In your classroom materials, you want to send a clear message that all students belong, and what they see upon entering classrooms and other school spaces will give them their first messages. Author and practitioner Debbie Miller asks us to set up our instructional spaces with intention, and by deliberately ensuring that our beliefs and practices are aligned.[3]

For this reason, you might consider: *What kinds of things are displayed in this teaching space? What type of student work is displayed if any? What do the materials say about the values of this classroom?*

Images, texts, signage, student work, district initiatives, and formal curricular resources all play a part in constructing the fiber of a classroom before any explicit instruction actually occurs. This is part of expanding our definition of a *text*. While we focus throughout this book on using literature for children to ground conversations, it is our belief that all of these materials matter.

One way that you can ensure that students are receiving messages that their identities and experiences matter in school spaces is to ensure that there are books (of course), images, videos, art, music, and accomplishments of people from different identity groups and backgrounds displayed visually as well as part of conversations. For example, highlighting prominent women of color in STEM (science, technology, engineering, and math) or leaders with disabilities can help ensure that all students feel included. In doing so, you set the stage to have discussions around different societal inequities that persist for particular identity groups.

THE ETHOS OF THE CLASSROOM/SOCIAL SPACE

Learning about Your Students

Any positive, warm, and curiosity-filled classroom environment will begin with learning about your students. There are inherent power dynamics in the teacher-student relationship, and we encourage you to take the stance that students bring knowledge, experience, and ideas that can help shape the classroom and learning. Freire reminds us that "it is in speaking their word that people, by naming the world, transform it."[4] We must offer students the opportunity to speak their truth and name their world. By listening and learning about the actual lives of students, we build a trusting community and find ways to meet students where they are. By having opportunities to speak their truth, students also develop a sense of agency and the confidence to enact change in their world, even from the youngest ages.

Author and longtime teacher Vivian Paley describes a curriculum for young students that is driven by their interests, lives, and the stories that they tell.[5] Through a playful study of picture books by Leo Lionni, the children learn to grapple with friendships, injustice, and identity through a familiar and beloved author. While structuring a unit flexibly around an author study may not be possible in your context, tapping into student experiences and what you know about your students can go a long way in helping them feel ownership over their classroom and learning. Literature and character can bring a playful element! Appendix B in this book includes sample discussion questions to use with literature, though we invite you to tailor your discussion questions to your students.

Learning about your students can be taken a step further by learning more about the community of your students. This is perhaps the most essential when you do not live in the community in which you teach. Liz Kleinrock, author of *Start Here, Start Now*, encourages educators to engage with community members to better understand the assets of the community and to bridge conversations between school and home for students.[6] Similarly, professor Maria Paula Ghiso argues that "schools themselves are transnational spaces," which she defines as twofold. First, there is the blurring of national boundaries (often seen through multiple dimensions of culture and language), common in communities with immigrant and multilingual families. Second, schools become transnational spaces when home and school boundaries become blended.[7] We can work to form these transnational spaces by strengthening our partnerships with caregivers and community members.

For example, consider visiting local businesses and restaurants to talk with people about their neighborhood, why they live there, and what they love about it. Bring those conversations into the classroom and invite students to contribute. As an educator, learning about these transnational spaces and welcoming the knowledge from student home lives into the classroom builds a foundation of trust and relevancy—priming your classroom community to have critical conversations. In addition, this demonstrates to students that their community is viewed as an asset, rather than a deficit (especially important in communities that have been underserved).

Tapping into families and caregivers through conversations, interest surveys, and input are additional ways to demonstrate to students and families that you are invested in building a classroom community that is reflective of all learners.

Carving Intentional Space for Community Building

While you build your knowledge of the community in which your classroom or educational setting is situated, you can simultaneously construct a community within your classroom that is safe and warm. One of the strategies for doing this is in having an intentional morning meeting. Rather than have students enter the classroom and begin working immediately, this morning meeting provides a soft start of connection. Consider how you begin your morning as adults—you may enter your workplace and say hello to your colleagues and get a cup of coffee. If you were expected to walk straight to your desk and dive into a new project that you had been assigned immediately, what tone would your day start with? If you saw a worksheet waiting on your desk, would you be excited to begin or would your face fall and body tense up? Many of our students crave the same—a gentle morning (perhaps where they can leisurely read from a book or draw) and then a time to gather as a class.

During a recent visit to a summer school kindergarten class, learning began with a morning meeting. The teacher had created an artificial campfire with logs and paper flames, and students sat around the campfire to check in with each other before starting their academic learning. A sense of calm and warmth filled the room as the students gathered in a daily circle around their campfire to share how they were feeling as they began the school day.

These morning meetings can take many forms. Often, teachers pose a question that helps students get to know one another. Others ask students to share how they are feeling that morning or to share personal news, or leave the meeting entirely open ended so that students can raise their own issues or questions for discussion. In some classrooms, teachers may have a consistent structure for a morning meeting.[8] As we will discuss later, teachers who have been engaging in identity work with their students (e.g., an identity profile) may carve out time for students to share their identity markers as they are comfortable during this designated time.

A distinction we want to make here is that morning meetings shouldn't be filled with scripted social-emotional lessons or generic questions. Rather, an authentic class meeting is constructed around the needs, interests, and experiences of the students, which demands more flexibility and responsiveness than pre-created lessons can provide. In fact, professor Rebecca Tilhou argues that morning meetings are democratic spaces where students can experience agency, active decision-making, and problem solving.[9] Students—not curriculum—should drive the conversation.

Pause & Reflect: How might you set up the routines of your classroom to ensure that a sense of community is evident?

Setting the Stage for Students to Share (Trust You, Trust Classroom)

Vulnerability builds trust, which in turn builds community. This work demands that we are all vulnerable, and sharing about your own identity can be a great way to model this with your students. For example, you might share with students the times that you struggled in school or didn't feel a sense of belonging. In turn, you give students the space to share about their lives.

Additionally, you might ask students to reflect and share how they feel during different class conversations—carving out space for emotional processing. Many teachers choose to do this by using tools such as the zones of regulation, where students can self-assess their emotions as they begin their school day.[10] Students need to trust that the classroom is a space where they can process their lived experiences, wrestle with social issues within the world, and be their authentic selves.[11] Where they can ask questions, and be honest if they are struggling. In primary classrooms, play can be leveraged as a mechanism for helping students develop their identities and gain empathy for one another. As Genishi and Dyson argue, play is "a socially complex communicative act," one in which students learn about themselves, their peers, and the world around them.[12] Through play, children act out different scenarios that help them to make sense of their peers, as well as learn to negotiate social relationships. This can build empathy and trust, as students learn to process alongside one another.

Pause & Reflect: Where are the spaces in your classroom or school where students can connect and build trusting relationships with one another?

As an educator, you can make guesses as to how your students are feeling in your classroom community, but you can't know for sure. Try paying attention to who speaks up in class discussions, and who does not. Note which students you have spent the most time conversing with—are those the same students who consistently speak up? Could your own biases or assumptions about students be impacting your relationship with them? This matters because we need to have a culture of sharing and trust before we can dive into identity and justice. If you want to be even more concrete, try having a colleague observe and take note of which students speak up in class discussion, or videotape a meeting or discussion to refer back to.

As Peter Johnston reminds us in *Choice Words*, our words matter.[13] How we talk about students and how we talk about learning are significant. Whether we are learning about identity and the world around us, or learning a new math concept, our beliefs and knowledge are never fixed. In front of students, model changing your mind about something when you learn more. Phrases such as, "I used to think _____, but since I've learned more, I now think ____" or "I made some assumptions about that person/character, but now I realize that my assumption was incorrect" open the door for students to revise their thinking too. Students may come to school with certain attitudes, biases, or misconceptions about groups of people, so modeling this language is even more important than ever. In the final chapter of this book, we discuss the importance of *calling in*, rather than calling out when having critical conversations, and this applies to both our colleagues as well as our students.[14]

Pause & Reflect: What indicators might you look for to determine whether your students feel comfortable sharing in your classroom? How might you collect input directly from your students on their comfort levels in sharing?

Trusting in Your Students

Many people don't give students enough credit. We share this belief that students are fully capable, interested, and ready to have difficult conversations, particularly conversations that impact them. We must remember that this next generation of students will lead our communities, and many of them have a strong desire to shape their world. They recognize injustice, and many are ready to speak out about this.

Professor Vivian Vasquez describes a situation where kindergarten students are excluded from a school-wide event, a French cafe, because they are young.[15] With support from the classroom teacher, these students create a petition to ask to be included in future school events. They see—and change—the reality of their participation at school through social action. Comber, Thomson, and Wells similarly examine how elementary students understand power and poverty in their local neighborhood, and leverage their writing to work against the injustices that they observe (in this case, neglect of a poor neighborhood).[16] These research projects demonstrate that even our youngest students see inequity and can advocate for change.

Rather than giving students a voice (which they already have), we can offer them a platform to share their ideas, thoughts, and experiences—showing them that their lived experiences, indeed, belong in a school setting and, in fact, add to the richness of school. Furthermore, the cultural and linguistic knowledge that our students (and their families) bring to educational settings can help create cultures of caring and belonging when tapped into, rather than overlooked.[17] This also includes holding space for the lived experiences that are often not discussed in school settings, such as incarcerated family members.[18]

Collaboratively Writing Agreements

A common beginning-of-year strategy in classrooms is to write community norms, or agreements that every member will follow. Involving students in the process reflects the teacher's respect for students' identities, shows that their voices are being heard and builds ownership in the process. Many educators are shifting from the language of "norms" to the language of "agreements" in efforts to avoid positioning dominant groups, culture, or behavior as standard or normal. Agreements refer to practices that the group has determined are important (these are different from expectations for behavior that a teacher may determine).

Glenn Singleton, in an interview at a high school in Illinois, reminds educators and community members that people of color (POC) regularly experience microaggressions, and these microaggressions add up.[19] There is a need for healing places within our school walls, so that students can process these experiences and learn from the experiences of others (if they are White, for example). The current default—yet unspoken—norm is that these issues are not discussed. In contrast, committing and agreeing to talk openly about identity markers in school settings can help provide these safe and healing spaces, and having agreements for how these issues are discussed can help ensure that the space is safe. We define and discuss microaggressions in depth in chapter 6.

We do advocate for collaboratively constructing agreements with students, with guidance and boundaries set by the teacher. For example, "assume positive intent" is a norm that is often used, but in sensitive conversations, the intent is not enough. Students also need to know that their impact matters, and we invite teachers to touch on the issues of intent versus impact, if age appropriate. Consider Singleton's suggested norms as you guide the development of your classroom agreements: stay engaged, speak your truth, experience discomfort, and expect and accept nonclosure.[20] Students will need support in understanding what these mean. Dr. Caprice Hollins and Ilsa Govan, in *Diversity, Equity, and Inclusion: Strategies for Facilitating Conversations on Race*, offer specific ideas for clarifying these norms.[21]

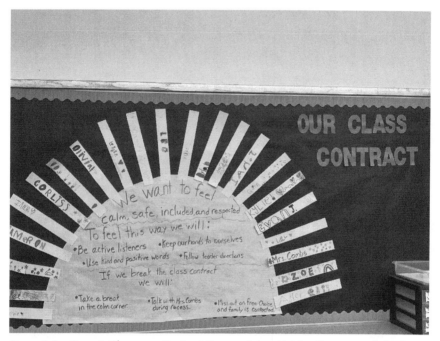

Figure 1.1.   Peggy's Classroom Contract Source: Arbor Heights Elementary School, Seattle

In a third-grade classroom, teacher Peggy shares her process in guiding the development of a class contract. During their regular morning class meetings, the class starts with brainstorming feeling words, then focuses on the question: "How do we want to feel in our class?" Next the class works together to identify what they would do in order to promote those types of feelings, and finally, what should happen when someone breaks the class contract. The completion of the class contract typically takes over a week to brainstorm, revise, and edit. In the photograph of their class contract, notice how the students each wrote their names on the rays of the sun, modeling shared ownership for the finished product.

One strategy for collaboratively developing agreements is to pose the questions: When we are sharing in ways that show respect for one another, "What does it look like? What does it sound like?" Additionally, teachers may choose to create a chart of sentence frames for conversations, such as: "I disagree because," "I agree with what _____ said, and want to add_____," and "When you said _____, I'm not sure what you meant."

Activities to Build Community

As you build your classroom community, there are popular activities that you might lean on. These activities have been conceptualized, created, and shared by others (some unknown), and we are grateful to be able to lean on these ideas.

"I Am From" Poems

These are beautiful, simple ways to have students share their backgrounds. This activity is built around George Ella Lyon's famous poem "Where I'm From," and students can be as vulnerable in their renditions as they choose.[22] "I Am From" poems typically have a template, so students will fill out different aspects of their lives, such as a family tradition, a meaningful object or smell, a song or family memento. After teachers model their own (or using someone else's poem), they can create and share a *flexible template* with some/all of the prompts below to give students guidance in shaping their poem in any order they choose.

I'm from (a location, city, community . . . where . . .)
I'm from (description of your home)
I'm from (an important item in your home or family)
I'm from (description of parents or other family members) . . . who . . .
I'm from (description of another family member) . . . who . . .
I'm from (weather you experience/experienced) . . . that . . .
I'm from (friendships, such as *I'm from a pretend sisters' club where we shared our fears and hopes*)
I'm from (memories of specific holidays)
I'm from (a plant, tree, or natural object that is/was important to you)
I'm from (a memory that stays with you)
I'm from (favorite music, foods, hobbies, games, vacations)
End with "That's where I'm from," or "That's where I'm from; where are you from?"

Bio Bags

Similarly, bio bags allow students to share who they are in a gentle and fun way. On the outside of a standard paper bag, students write or draw the identity markers that are visible (e.g., I am a female, and I am an educator). On the inside, students write or draw cards that illustrate the more invisible components of their identity, things that you wouldn't know just by looking at them. For example, a student might write that they are vegetarian and place this inside their bag. An alternative is to invite students to place objects that represent these aspects of identity inside the bag, such as a cultural or family memento or photograph. This opens up complex conversations about what identity is, and the dangers of making assumptions about a person strictly based on their visible identity markers or outside appearance.

Identity Iceberg

As you unpack these experiences with students, it might be helpful to provide a visual, such as the identity iceberg. The identity iceberg is a wonderful representation that demonstrates visible identity markers (above the waterline), and a much larger group of invisible identity markers (below the waterline). This visual, alongside some of the other activities, can help remind students that identities are multifaceted. Emilie and Pamela have included their own personal identity icebergs as examples.

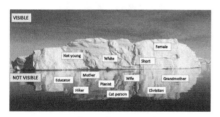

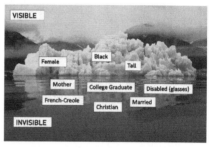

Figure 1.2 Emilie's Identity Iceberg Example   Source: Emilie Hard

Figure 1.3 Pamela's Identity Iceberg Example   Source: Pamela Washington

Identity Profiles

This is an activity that was used at Renton Park Elementary, where Pamela is the principal. As Pamela reflects on her educational experiences as a Black woman, what stands out is the absence of opportunity to celebrate the uniqueness she brought to the learning environments as well as the opportunities to learn about others different from herself. As a result, she succumbed to the dominant culture around her, resulting in assimilating into what she perceived as the "right way"—Whiteness. In the timely and much-needed book *Identity Affirming Classrooms: Spaces That Center Humanity*, Erica Buchanan-Rivera speaks to the urgency of educators creating spaces that affirm the racial identities of students in their learning communities.[23] One way to do this is through exploring perceptions about identity through self-portraits. In partnership with Edutopia, Shana White unpacks a student-friendly identity activity that can be conducted with students K–12.[24] This activity opens the discussion within your community of learners to explore similarities and differences between classmates while authentically stepping in as their authentic selves. Pamela is proud that all K–5 Renton Park staff, including special education staff, chose to do this activity with their students, which speaks to the sense of urgency that we all have about creating a sense of belonging for our students. Included is a student example.

Teachers may want to offer choices about how students communicate their identity profiles—posters, digital presentations, artifact boxes, and poems are a few possibilities.

Figure 1.4. Sample Student Identity Profile   Source: Renton Park Elementary School, Renton

Examining Classroom and School Traditions

In addition to the classroom- or school-based activities mentioned above, it's essential that schools examine some long-standing traditions from a critical lens. Many educational institutions have moved away from centering Christmas during the month of December, for example, in favor of showcasing all the different religious and cultural holidays that occur throughout the winter months. This is certainly a start, but it is not sufficient.

To celebrate diversity and culture in our school buildings, many implement cultural celebration nights. Families might set up different booths or bring food, artifacts, and clothing to celebrate their culture. We offer just a word of caution on these types of events, as they can make culture seem like a token if not done intentionally. Find ways to widen and shift these traditions so that celebrating heritage applies and is relevant to all students, not just those who come from the nondominant culture.

Other school traditions, such as spirit days, may deserve some examination from an inclusion and belonging lens. Do the spirit days celebrated in your school allow students to express who they are, or do they encourage conformity? An example of a spirit day that promotes belonging is "You Be You Day," where students are invited to dress in a way that reflects who they are (this may be a costume, a shirt with an appropriate message, a traditional cultural outfit, etc.). This can be contrasted with "Team Day" or "Jersey Day" where students who don't connect with sports may not be inclined to participate or could feel left out.

Language Used in Everyday Conversations Matters

While activities and intentional moments can go a long way toward creating a positive and warm classroom community, the language used every day also deserves our attention. Of course, some of the language used in classrooms comes from our materials and curriculum guides—this is the language of the formal curriculum. For example, "turn and talk" is a phrase common in many elementary classrooms that refers to a particular instructional strategy and routine for response.

Gerald Campano, literacy professor and researcher, describes an ideological space in the classroom that is outside of the formal curriculum.[25] This space might be during transitions, during independent work time, while helping students solve problems, or other minutes of the day where you are not instructing. Here, in these moments, conversation is more fluid and informal—and it is a space rich with possibilities for forming connections. It is also a space where our language matters, because students are taking cues from us about the values of school and formal educational spaces.

Similarly, Peter Johnston asks us to attend to our language in both formal and informal teaching. As educators, we often attend to our formal language, but it is easy to let our guard down during more informal times. He articulates that language "actually creates realities and invites identities,", leaving no doubt about the power of our words.[26] He provides the example that telling a student "You are so smart" is different from "You are so thoughtful" as the latter asks students to see themselves as part of a community, and as someone who can impact the lives of others. Both comments are valuable and have good intentions. However, we invite you to be mindful about the impact that your word choices may have. This is even more critical when it comes to our language as we discuss diversity. Ensuring that specific cultures and identity groups are discussed from an asset lens matters both to students who have those identity markers, as well as those who do not.

Asking students what they *notice* and *wonder* increases the agency and ownership with which they might approach a task. Encouraging students to *imagine* how one another (or a character) feels in particular

> Pause & Reflect: How does the everyday language of your classroom affirm student identities and experience?

scenarios builds empathy. Similarly, asking students to *solve problems collectively*—and then articulate how they were able to do so—instills a sense of community collaboration in students beyond what a formal curriculum guide may offer.

HIGH EXPECTATIONS FOR ALL STUDENTS

When considering the atmosphere of your classroom and building community with students, it's important to maintain high expectations for all students—in fact, these high expectations will also add to the culture of your classroom. Zaretta Hammond and others refer to this as the "warm demander" approach, where teachers focus on emotional support, scaffolding, and high expectations for student achievement.[27] There is a primary emphasis on fostering relationships and because of this, teachers are able to provide tough love, encourage productive struggle, and expect rigor. High expectations create environments for intellectual curiosity, questioning, and learning that is relevant. While maintaining high expectations, it may be essential to also provide scaffolds and accessibility to students to ensure that they have the tools to meet these expectations. The best part is, this often begins with trust, but it subsequently builds trust.

Part of creating community (both with colleagues and with students) is a commitment to continually learning. We are continually learning in this work, and our own identities therefore greatly inform this work and process. As educators and coauthors, we ruminate on these issues in our own professional contexts, as well as with one another. We are grateful for the partnership and community that we have with like-minded colleagues—the teachers featured in this book.

By sharing our own identities, stories, and experiences, we work to build vulnerability and trust, as well as expand our own knowledge of varying school experiences. In the words of Dr. Damien Pattenaude, superintendent of Renton School District, "Whatever space students walk into, they should feel welcomed, affirmed and loved." Join us as we commit to disrupting the assumptions, biases, and misconceptions that we bring to this work.

Pause & Reflect: Are the building blocks there for you to begin facilitating critical conversations with your students? How will you begin constructing this foundation? And experience?

SUMMARY OF KEY POINTS FROM THIS CHAPTER

- It is essential that teachers create a classroom culture that is conducive to community, inquiry, and empathy.
- Ensure that the physical and social space are supportive, safe places that promote belonging for each person.
- Vulnerability builds trust and community.
- Trust your students by demonstrating that their voices add to the richness of the learning.
- Consider developing classroom agreements in collaboration with your students.
- Build community with activities such as bio bags, identity icebergs, and "I Am From" poems.
- Examine your classroom and school traditions with an equity lens.
- Be mindful of the impact of the language you use with students.
- Hold high expectations for all students.

SUGGESTED PICTURE BOOK LIST: CLASSROOM COMMUNITIES

- *Be You!* by Peter Reynolds (2020)
- *Each Kindness* by Jacqueline Woodson (2012)
- *I'm New Here* by Ann Sibley O'Brien (2018)
- *Maybe Something Beautiful: How Art Transformed a Neighborhood* by F. Isabel Campoy and Theresa Howell (2016)
- *The Invisible Boy* by Trudy Ludwig and Patrice Barton (2013)
- *This Is a School* by John Schu (2022)
- *We All Belong: A Children's Book about Diversity, Race and Empathy* by Nathalie Goss (2022)
- *What's My Superpower?* by Aviaq Johnston (2017)
- *Where Are You From?* by Yamile Saied Mendez (2019)

NOTES

1. Brown, B. (2015). *Daring greatly: How the courage to be vulnerable transforms the way we live, love, parent, and lead*, pp. 231–232. New York: Avery.
2. Freire, P. (1970). *Pedagogy of the oppressed*. London: Penguin.
3. Miller, D. (2008). *Teaching with intention: Defining beliefs, aligning practice, taking action*. Portland, ME: Stenhouse.
4. Freire, P. (1970). *Pedagogy of the oppressed*, p. 69. London: Penguin.

5. Paley, V. (1998). *The girl with the brown crayon: How children use stories to shape their lives.* Cambridge, MA: Harvard University Press.

6. Kleinrock, L. (2021). *Start here, start now: A guide to antibias and antiracist work in your school community.* Portsmouth, NH: Heinemann.

7. Ghiso, M. P. (2016). The laundromat as the transnational local: Young children's literacies of interdependence. *Teachers College Record, 118*(1), 1–46.

8. Kriete, R., & Davis, C. (2014). *The morning meeting book.* Turners Falls, MA: Center for Responsive Schools.

9. Tilhou, R. C. (2020). The morning meeting: Fostering a participatory democracy begins with youth in public education. *Democracy & Education, 28*(2), 1–11. Retrieved from https://democracyeducationjournal.org/home/vol28/iss2/5/

10. Kuypers, L. (2011). *Zones of regulation: A curriculum designed to foster self -regulation and emotional control.* San Jose, CA: Think Social.

11. Jones, S. (2006). *Girls, social class, and literacy: What teachers can do to make a difference.* Portsmouth, NH: Heinemann.

12. Genishi, C., & Dyson, A. H. (2009). *Children, language, and literacy: Diverse learners in diverse times,* p. 61. New York: Teachers College Press.

13. Johnston, P. (2004). *Choice words.* Portland, ME: Stenhouse.

14. Ross, L. (2021). *Don't call people out—call them in* [Video]. TED talk. Retrieved from https://www.youtube.com/watch?v=xw_720iqdss

15. Vasquez, V. (2001). Constructing a critical curriculum with young children. In B. Comber & A. Simpson (Eds.), *Negotiating critical literacies in classrooms.* London: Routledge.

16. Comber, B., Thomson, P., & Wells, M. (2001). Critical literacy finds a "place": Writing and social action in a low-income Australian grade 2/3 classroom. *Elementary School Journal, 101*(4), 451–464.

17. Campano, G., Ghiso, M. P., & Welch, B. J. (2016). *Partnering with immigrant communities: Action through literacy.* New York: Teachers College Press.

18. Jones, S. (2006). *Girls, social class, and literacy: What teachers can do to make a difference.* Portsmouth, NH: Heinemann.

19. Sparks, D. (2002, Fall). Conversations about race need to be fearless: A conversation with Glenn Singleton. *Journal of Staff Development, 23*(4). Retrieved from https://intranet.oprfhs.org/board-of-education/board_meetings/Special_Meetings/Packets/2007/020908.pdf

20. Singleton, G. (2015). *Courageous conversations about race: A field guide for achieving equity in schools.* Thousand Oaks, CA: Corwin.

21. Hollins, C., & Govan, I. (2015). *Diversity, equity, and inclusion: Strategies for facilitating conversations on race.* Lanham, MD: Rowman & Littlefield.

22. Lyon, G. E. (1999). *Where I'm from: Where poems come from.* Spring, TX: Absey.

23. Buchanan-Rivera, E. (2022). *Identity affirming classrooms: Spaces that center humanity.* London: Routledge.

24. White, S. (2019). *Creating a learning environment where all kids feel valued.* Edutopia. Retrieved from https://www.edutopia.org/article/creating-learning -environment-where-all-kids-feel-valued

25. Campano, G. (2006). *Immigrant students and literacy: Reading, writing, and remembering.* New York: Teachers College Press.

26. Johnston, P. (2004). *Choice words*, p. 9. Portland, ME: Stenhouse.

27. Hammond, Z. (2014). *Culturally responsive teaching and the brain: Promoting authentic engagement and rigor among culturally and linguistically diverse students.* Thousand Oaks, CA: Corwin.

2

✛

Identity and Belonging
Student Understanding of Self

Reeny uses markers for the dress, the hair, or even to outline the body, but the face, arms, hands, and legs are carefully colored in with a brown crayon, which she removes from the box as soon as she sits down. There it stays on the paper, ready to certify: This girl is brown like me.—Vivian Paley[1]

For most people, learning is a social endeavor. Children come to school to learn, but in order to learn, a sense of belonging and connection must be present. This belonging allows students to make healthy connections, and to feel that they are an integral part of their school and class community. This is more essential than ever; students and teachers alike wrestle with ongoing trauma from the pandemic amid new curricula and instructional delivery methods, renewed assessment, political factors, and safety concerns.

As we strive to create a sense of belonging for each student, one of our goals must be to leverage the talent and the intellect in our students' identities and foster these opportunities for greatness within our classrooms.[2] Not only does this strength-based approach help students see their gifts and develop agency, but it also builds a foundation for acknowledging and appreciating the strengths of others—key to an inclusive community where all students belong.

What follows in this chapter are several snapshots of how teachers have chosen to approach conversations around identity with students through an asset lens. While we define text as broad, we do lean on picture books as a source of information and connection in elementary classrooms. This chapter will focus twofold on using texts as "mirrors" for the purpose of helping students deepen their understanding of themselves, as well as integrating the language of mirrors as a foundation for identity discussions. Subsequent chapters will build on these conversations, asking students to read for the purpose of understanding new perspectives, and finally, to consider the ways that they might enact change in their communities.

As you read the examples, we invite you to stop and reflect on how you might modify or extend conversations on these topics with your own students in a way that is meaningful for your learners. Importantly, these snapshots capture a brief moment in time, yet these teachers are committed to discussing identity with their students on a much larger scale. Therefore, the snapshots here do not operate in isolation.

At the end of the book, we include a resource with discussion prompts to use with picture books that support identity, empathy, and advocacy.

VISIBLE AND INVISIBLE IDENTITY MARKERS: FIRST GRADE WITH TORI

What this teacher's lesson intends to do is help young students apply what they have noticed in the real world to texts and to take a more analytical lens to representation in literature. This snapshot supports student understanding of their own identities through mirror texts. Later lessons in this classroom will help students recognize the identities and experiences of others through windows. From there, students will be able to identify whether a specific text is a mirror or window for them, which will assist them in selecting texts, deepening an understanding of character, and developing empathy for others with a foundation of belonging.

Using the social justice standards put forth by the organization Learning for Justice can assist you in anchoring your discussions. The lesson that follows would address Identity Anchor Standard 1: "Students will develop positive social identities based on their membership in multiple groups in society," as well as Identity Anchor Standard 4: "Students will express pride, confidence and healthy self-esteem without denying the value and dignity of other people."[3]

This first-grade lesson integrates the vocabulary of mirrors for students and encourages them to home in on the reflections of themselves. This vocabulary may inform their text selections, as well as reaffirm to students that they deserve to be represented in the texts across their classroom and school. This, in turn, can fuel a positive identity as well as a sense of agency.

Tori, the classroom teacher, asks students to notice the visible parts of their own identity (their race, gender, appearance), as well as the aspects of their identity that are beneath the surface (hobbies, family traditions, fears, personality traits). The class discusses what "tool" they could use to complete their portrait, and they settle on mirrors. The class brainstorms what they might see when they look in their mirror, things like: hair, face, eyes and eyebrows, ears, and mask (as we are still in pandemic-style learning at this time). Students also consider the "hidden" parts of themselves, and create a self-portrait.

The class has recently completed "I Am From" poems (see previous chapter). Reflecting on these poems, Tori connects prior learning to new learning: "Those poems are about the inside of you. Today, we're going to use a mirror to see the outside of you!" Since this lesson occurs during the pandemic, she emphasizes that some students might choose to draw the mask they are wearing, and others might picture what their smile looks like and draw that. Tori asks, "Do you have a dimple when you smile? Draw that detail!" Students are encouraged to honor the ways that they look.

Students select a small bin of mixed *people color* crayons to use. Students are invited to select an entire bin, choose just one, and/or use the materials they already have at their desks. Tori asks students to use any and all materials at their disposal to represent themselves. These crayons are popular; however, what we want to draw attention to here is the intentional conversations around skin color. Tori models selecting a crayon for her own self-portrait for students by holding up a few different colors until she finds one that is close to her skin tone. The idea that each individual self-selects their own skin tone crayon is an important concept that Tori has discussed with both students and other teachers. She believes firmly in the importance of students making their own determination of their skin color, and has candid conversations with her students about not telling other people what color crayon they should choose. When having conversations around identity, it's essential that all students feel empowered to name who they are, rather than having identity markers (such as a particular racial or ethnic group) imposed on them.

Tori models starting her own portrait as students gather materials. She draws a scar in her eyebrow to highlight that people can see it (outside) but they may not know why it's there (inside). In drawing attention to this example, she is previewing for students the idea that our identities are a combination of what we see when we look at ourselves, coupled with internal traits, dreams, experiences, and fears. Therefore, we can never know a person simply by looking at them. Students start their portraits and begin talking about their eye color. "My eyes are brown" and "My eyes are black!" are audible statements. For primary students, drawing attention to these concrete observations is essential.

The students pause their portraits and gather for a story; Tori is using this as an opportune time to bring in some discussion about mirrors and representation. Before starting the story, Tori explains that when we have these types of discussions, everyone gets to decide for themselves what they look like, what color their eyes are, or what kind of hair they have.

Pause & Reflect: How might you set the stage for this conversation, given your knowledge of your students?

In addition to noticing visible aspects of identity, Tori extends the discussion to invisible identity factors. Tori shares her example of being adopted into a family where there are few visible similarities between herself and her family members. Her skin color is different from her family members; however, they have common characteristics and experiences, things you wouldn't necessarily understand simply by looking at them.

Tori shares: "We just looked at the outside of ourselves with mirrors. Sometimes when we read books, there are characters that are like us in ways that you can't see on the outside. This is a book about a bird, so it doesn't look like me. But, this book is a really big mirror for me." This helps students understand that there are many ways that we might feel represented in books, as our identities are multifaceted. A mirror text can be a mirror text for a variety of reasons. Teachers can model this concept by sharing parts of themselves with their students, as Tori does here, and explain how different texts offer connections to their visible identity or the more nuanced parts.

One student responds to a section of the book where a mother bear adopts a bird by observing: "They look so different." Tori acknowledges the student's comment (the animals do indeed look physically different), and then explains why this book is a mirror for her. The character (the bird) is trying to find people who look like him in his family. In doing so, the bird realizes an important lesson—that they don't need to look like him in order to be his family.

"Do you remember the picture that I showed you of my parents?" Students nod, and Tori explains that they are a family even though they don't look alike or have the same skin color. This discussion could then be extrapolated to other ways that families might be different from one another (such as single parent, LGBTQIA+ parents, divorced parents, etc.). Tori plants the seed that we can represent the visible aspects of ourselves through self-portraits, but we can also find literature that is reflective of our less visible characteristics. What is most important is that each person sees themselves as belonging in many different places.[4]

Pause & Reflect: What additional strategies can you think of for responding to the student's comment "They look so different"? How can you use texts to deepen your students' understanding of identity?

By no means is this scenario the only way to accomplish these types of goals. Whether you have students engage with a portrait, discussion, or something else entirely, having students consider the inside and outside components of their identity while building a sense of confidence and belonging is important. This lesson is just the beginning, and sets the stage for language and practices that are consistent in Tori's classroom.

NAMES AS CENTRAL TO OUR IDENTITY: SECOND GRADE WITH STACEY

Another aspect of identity teachers may want to explore with students is names. For many, names can be a reflection of our cultural, ethnic, or religious heritage. Taking the time to understand student names—and have students understand the names of their peers—is an important step in constructing an inclusive and empathetic classroom community.

Fortunately, the publishing world has attended to this focus, with picture books specifically highlighting characters who encounter difficulty related to their name. Books such as *Always Anjali* by Sheetal Sheth and *Your Name Is a Song* by Jamilah Thompkins-Bigelow can serve as mirrors for students who have names that might be considered unique in their school context.[5]

Second-grade teacher Stacey chooses to use a familiar text for students, *The Name Jar*, to open a conversation around names at the beginning of the year with an intention to build understanding and respect among her students.[6] Learning about names often leads to conversations about family traditions and culture. Therefore, this text and discussion supports Learning for Justice's Identity Anchor Standard 4: "Students will express pride, confidence and healthy self-esteem without denying the value and dignity of other people," as well as Diversity Anchor Standard 8: Students will respectively express curiosity about the history and lived experiences of others and will exchange ideas and beliefs in an open-minded way."[7]

Throughout the read-aloud, Stacey makes deliberate connections to her students' own lives to extend the conversation, asking them to reflect on their names as well as the names of their classmates and friends.

As the character in the text (Unhei) is introduced, a student comments: "I have a friend who's Japanese and sometimes I get her name wrong." Another student agrees that this too had happened to her. Importantly, these comments are met with empathy rather than judgment, which develops the discussion further. These comments are crucial because the students are not only making connections to their own lives, but they are subtly reflecting on the potential impact of mispronouncing someone else's name. By validating these statements, yet nudging students to think more critically about their actions, Stacey teaches students that it's important to learn from mistakes we make in order to improve the way we treat one another.

In response to her classmates, another student suggests: "I think you should ask a person what their name is, and then find help learning how to pronounce it." A second student comments by sharing: "Once on TV I saw a person who asked someone how to pronounce their name and they spelled it. So that could help to learn it and be friends." These comments demonstrate how students learn new strategies for forming connections with one another, and for treating all with respect.

Pause & Reflect: How might you respond to the comments shared by students in the above section?

As the text progresses into a resolution, where the character Unhei begins to feel proud of her name, a student recognizes: "She's [Unhei's mother] trying to make her feel better to make her feel special." Similarly, another chimes in: "She wants Unhei to be happy about being different." With help from Stacey, students recognize and verbalize that having a unique name is something to be celebrated. A seemingly simple concept, this realization is more powerful when generated collectively, rather than as a statement made by the teacher.

Later on, Stacey guides students to understand that it's important to appreciate the differences that we all have. A student states: "People ARE different, and it's okay to have different names" to show his understanding of the book's main message. Stories like this that help students to see the character's perspectives and feelings can provide an access point for application to the broader world. In this example, the student recognizes that our names reflect the reality of who we are—that we are all unique. To respect this uniqueness, we must also respect our names.

The goal is that students gain a sense of empathy through learning about the experiences of others and to ensure that each student feels that their unique experiences and attributes belong in the classroom. We see this multiple times with student responses, who are using the read-aloud as a springboard to reflect on their own lives and friendships. While this text may be a window for some students, it is a mirror for other students who have names that may be unfamiliar to their peers.

STUDENT OWNERSHIP IN THE CLASSROOM LIBRARY: FOURTH GRADE WITH MADYSON

The next snapshot occurs in fourth grade, and demonstrates how student thinking becomes deeper as students have more experience with these types of conversations. Importantly, these discussions do not function in isolation—in fact, each week, this teacher carves out intentional time to have conversations around identity as a component of social-emotional learning. However, each conversation with students is powerful on its own. In addition, the instructional coach at this school has partnered with teachers to plan read-alouds with deliberate discussion in efforts to showcase a variety of diverse texts. This is productive in promoting consistent language across classrooms.

This lesson addresses Learning for Justice's Identity Anchor Standard 3, "Students will recognize that people's multiple identities interact and create unique and complex individuals," and Identity Anchor Standard 4: Students will express pride, confidence and healthy self-esteem without denying the value and dignity of other people."[8] This teacher selects the book and activity that follows for the purposes of celebrating our complex identities, respecting others in a classroom community, and giving students a voice in the texts at their disposal.

This teacher, Madyson, has engaged students in art projects ("I Am From" poems, identity maps) and discussions about identity. She participates in a "book-a-day" routine, which incorporates a book with diverse representation into her classroom each day. The culture of the school, as well as the racial and ethnic diversity, has created a commitment to equity, making these types of projects more widespread. These discussions are tied to character analysis, evidenced by charts comparing/contrasting characters in their class texts, and another brainstorming chart titled "What Makes People Different and Diverse?" Intentionally tying these discussions to standards and curricula, as well as strategically building vocabulary around equity and inclusion, are deliberate choices here.

Madyson wants these conversations to continue to dig deeper to help students move beyond thinking of identity as their favorite food or hobby, but instead to think of identities as multifaceted and layered, such as personality traits (shy, kind, adventurous) and group affiliations (religion, neighborhood). This becomes more feasible at the intermediate level when students have experience with these conversations from prior years.

Leveraging Literature to Talk about Race

The picture book *Let's Talk about Race* is intended to help students see that we all have stories about who we are, and those stories are key to our identities.[9] Sometimes, the stories students have heard about their race—in particular—are negative. The book also tackles stereotypes, arguing instead that "none of these stories are true." While celebrating our individual identities, this book also highlights our collective humanity.

Madyson opens the conversation by reminding students that they have been discussing race, and how race is one facet of our identity. She talks about how much she is learning from the students and their experiences, which is a key in building trust and ensuring that each student feels that they have a voice in the classroom.

Madyson asks students to consider the impact of focusing on only a visible aspect of our identity (such as race), rather than the other facets of our identities. Students state that we would "miss out" and that we might "judge people based on what they look like before getting to know them." Some of the students' conversations become passionate at this point, with students feeling strongly that race or gender should not be a categorization in which people are judged.

Rather than read the text herself, Madyson chooses to show a video of the rapper and producer Common reading the book. This is an intentional choice to have a person of color featured, rather than herself (Madyson identifies as White). She is transparent with students about this intentional choice and desire to show POC in various roles. This is an important shift in practice in all content areas, particularly where POC, LGBTQIA+, and female individuals are underrepresented.

Common, while reading, emphasizes that there are things about him that you wouldn't know by looking at him (an example is that he is a vegetarian). The students pair up to share something about themselves beyond what they look like, and are invited to share whatever they are comfortable with. Some students share their fears. Like our first-grade snapshot, these students are considering identity as multifaceted, both the visible components of identity as well as the less apparent aspects.

Giving Students a Voice in Your Classroom Library

Later on, Madyson raises the concept of mirrors and windows in literature, terms that these students are familiar with. She places around the room tiny piles of chapter books for students to peruse while using sticky notes to identify whether the book is a mirror or window. The purpose of this activity is twofold:

1. Students will find books they love.
2. Students will identify books that serve as mirrors and windows for them.

Madyson frames this task by sharing: "I want to learn about our class library, to see if there are mirror books for every member of our class community. Our school is changing, and I want to know if our library has changed, too." While improving her classroom library, Madyson also gives students an authentic task through which to explore representation in literature. Even more so, she is diversifying her classroom library by asking for their input—not making assumptions on what students might consider to be mirror texts.

Students peruse the books. Midway through, Madyson stops the class and asks them to raise their hand if they haven't yet found a mirror book. Several students raise their hands. She asks: "What are you looking for in a mirror?" All answers are accepted.

One student in particular responds: "A girl who starts a new school and is behind, like me." Another student wants to find a character who is from India. The teacher leads her to books that she agrees are mirrors, after sifting through the pile. However, this particular student also writes "mirror" on *Alice in Wonderland*.[10] When discussing her choice, she states that she is adventurous, like Alice.

What emerges is that students vacillate between various aspects of their identity when exploring the books. They bring these different components (being from India; being adventurous) to bear when selecting texts, and each of these components is seen as valuable.

At the end of this activity, Madyson emphasizes that she will use this knowledge to examine her classroom library. Every student deserves to have mirrors, and she promises that she will take their statements into

Pause & Reflect: How can (or how do) students have a voice in your classroom library? In what ways does this lesson support a sense of belonging for Madyson's students?

account and the class library will continue to grow and change to match their needs.

ARTICULATING MIRRORS AND WINDOWS TO BUILD CLASS COMMUNITY: FIRST GRADE WITH ANNIE

In a similar lesson, first-grade teacher Annie discusses mirrors and windows with students. She highlights that a window text might be considered a window text because it's an experience that the student has not had. Interestingly, during this lesson students primarily identify mirrors and windows by internal aspects of their identity (experiences, traditions, and hobbies) rather than whether or not they visibly resemble the characters in the book. The teacher nudges students to consider the visible aspects of identity as well, modeling her own vulnerability with Joanna Ho's book *Eyes That Kiss in the Corners* and growing up knowing her eyes looked different than those of her peers.[11]

After identifying mirror and window books, students use a digital platform to record videos of themselves sharing a mirror book with an explanation of why that book reflects their identity and/or experience. Students articulate statements such as: "A mirror book is a book that you can see yourself in and it's really important. Then, a window is something you can't see yourself in but you can see someone else." Another student comments: "A window is something you haven't experienced, but a mirror is something you have experienced." Students post these videos to their online class journal, where classmates can view each other's to better build class community, as well as learn more about one another. By articulating these definitions, students deepen their understanding that classrooms are spaces where all students belong.

Pause & Reflect: What strategies might you use to determine students' level of understanding of mirrors and windows?

Inviting students to have a voice in your classroom (or school) library can happen at all grade levels, as these snapshots show. This gives students an authentic purpose for identifying mirrors and windows, and can provide a sense of agency.

Engaging in discussions with students about mirror texts can not only validate student identities as assets, but also build a foundation for these conversations to develop in the future. Understanding one's own identity and the identities of others can nurture the development of empathy as well as foster a sense of belonging for each student. Finally, these dispositions can inspire students to take action in creating social change, which will be the focus of chapter 4.

Pause & Reflect: What ideas do you have to nurture identity and a sense of belonging for each of your students?

This quote by Bettina L. Love (from the foreword in Gholdy Muhammad's *Cultivating Genius*) sums up the importance of providing a classroom and school environment where students can explore their identity: "You must know who you are and why you are important to this world, and learn how to be you. And this is particularly true for our Black and Brown children—because this world will constantly tell you that you are not good enough based on the color of your skin."[12] Using texts that highlight identity, teaching the meaning of mirrors and windows, and supporting students in expanding their understanding of their own identities provide the foundation for next steps in teaching and demonstrating empathy.

SUMMARY OF KEY POINTS FROM THIS CHAPTER

- A sense of belonging must be present in order to learn effectively.
- "Mirror" texts can help students cultivate a positive sense of identity.
- Provide opportunities for students to identify their own mirror books.
- With students, explore the visible aspects of identity as well as those that are not physically seen.
- Help students name their own identity markers, rather than imposing their identity on them.
- Names are an important part of student identity and deserve attention.

SUGGESTED PICTURE BOOK LIST: IDENTITY AND BELONGING

Note: The suggested books for chapters 2 and 3 can be interchangeable, as what is a mirror for one child might be a window for another.

- *A Different Pond* by Bao Phi (2017)
- *Alma and How She Got Her Name* by Juana Martinez-Neal (2018)
- *American Desi* by Jyoti Rajan Gopal (2022)
- *Black Gold* by Laura Obuobi (2022)
- *Bubbie & Rivka's Best-Ever Challah (So Far!)* by Sarah Lynne Reul (2022)
- *Cece Loves Science* by Kimberly Derting and Shelli R. Johannes (2020)
- *Cora Cooks Pancit* by Dorina K. Lazo Gilmore (2014)
- *Daddy, Papa and Me* by Leslea Newman (2008)
- *Eyes That Kiss in the Corners* by Joanna Ho (2021)
- *Eyes That Speak to the Stars* by Joanna Ho (2022)
- *Ginny and Kvetch* by Caroline Prichard (2021)
- *Heather Has 2 Mommies* by Leslea Newman (2016)
- *I Can Be All Three* by Salima Alikhan (2023)
- *In Our Mothers' House* by Patricia Polacco (2009)
- *Isabel and Her Colores Go to School* by Alexandra Alessandri (2021)
- *My Papi Has a Motorcycle* by Isabel Quintero (2019)
- *Nigel and the Moon* by Antwan Eady (2022)
- *Sulwe* by Lupita Nyong'o (2019)
- *Teddy's Favorite Toy* by Christian Trimmer (2018)
- *The Day You Begin* by Jacqueline Woodson (2018)
- *The Proudest Blue* by Ibtihaj Muhammad (2019)
- *The Year We Learned to Fly* by Jacqueline Woodson (2022)
- *Watercress* by Andrea Wang (2021)
- *What Does Brown Mean to You?* by Ron Grady (2023)
- *When Rubin Plays* by Gracey Zhang (2023)
- *Where Three Oceans Meet* by Rajani LaRocca (2021)
- *Yo Soy Muslim: A Father's Letter to His Daughter* by Mark Gonzales (2017)
- *Your Name Is a Song* by Jamilah Thompkins-Bigelow (2020)

NOTES

1. Paley, V. (1998). *The girl with the brown crayon: How children use stories to shape their lives*, p. 2. Cambridge, MA: Harvard University Press.

2. Muhammad, G. (2020). *Cultivating genius: An equity framework for culturally and historically responsive literacy.* New York: Scholastic.

3. Southern Poverty Law Center (2021). *Frameworks.* Learning for Justice. Retrieved from https://www.learningforjustice.org/frameworks

4. Johnston, P. (2004). *Choice words.* Portland, ME: Stenhouse.

5. Sheth, S. (2018). *Always Anjali.* Cambridge, MA: Mango & Marigold. Thompkins-Bigelow, J. (2020). *Your name is a song.* Seattle, WA: Innovation.

6. Choi, Y. (2003). *The name jar.* New York: Dragonfly Books.

7. Southern Poverty Law Center (2021). *Frameworks.* Learning for Justice. Retrieved from https://www.learningforjustice.org/frameworks

8. Southern Poverty Law Center (2021). *Frameworks.* Learning for Justice. Retrieved from https://www.learningforjustice.org/frameworks

9. Lester, J. (2008). *Let's talk about race.* New York: HarperCollins.

10. Carroll, L. (1981). *Alice's adventures in wonderland and through the looking -glass.* New York: Bantam Classics.

11. Ho, J. (2021). *Eyes that kiss in the corners.* New York: HarperCollins.

12. Muhammad, G. (2020). *Cultivating genius: An equity framework for culturally and historically responsive literacy.* New York: Scholastic.

3

Knowledge, Perspective, and Empathy

Understanding Others

When we speak of listening with understanding and empathy, we are really talking of transcending generations of ethnocentrism to truly see and value the abundant diversity of other cultures, races, religions, language systems, political systems, and economic views to develop a more stable world community.—Arthur L. Costa and Bena Kallick[1]

This chapter builds on the conversations that students have been having around identity by asking them to take on new perspectives; specifically, in using texts as a *window* into a character's background, culture, or experience. The goal of these discussions is to nudge students toward more nuanced thinking about others while subsequently building empathy. Following lines of thinking from Chimamanda Adichie, the power of window texts is in providing multiple narratives.[2] Teachers use these texts to celebrate differences and reinforce the value of showing respect for all people.

With texts such as Angela Kunkel's *Digging for Words: Jose Alberto Gutierrez and the Library He Built*, students have a window into someone's life and culture.[3] This gives students an opportunity to learn about implicit biases and stereotypes, and to consider what connects diverse people and underscores collective experiences. *The 1619 Project: Born on the Water*, for example, may assist students in exploring the nuances for those whose ancestors were enslaved, offering a powerful forum for understanding racial histories.[4]

CAN EMPATHY BE TAUGHT?

The Habits of Mind (HoM) research and publications of Dr. Arthur Costa and Dr. Bena Kallick had a profound influence on Emilie's educational journey. Their Institute for Habits of Mind promotes the direct teaching, practicing, valuing, and infusing of the HoM into classroom and school culture.[5] During Emilie's ten years as the principal at Glacier Park Elementary, the HoM were infused into curricula and instruction, and one of the HoM was identified as a school-wide focus for each month. Assemblies with HoM skits, songs, and activities promoted deep understanding of the habits. The school-wide focus allowed for the HoM to become a centerpiece of the school culture. Costa and Kallick define empathy as listening to understand others. We expand on that definition to include empathy as being open to understanding another person's point of view.[6] Empathy is one of the HoM that is a vital component of social-emotional learning. It enables students to strengthen relationships, resolve conflicts, and become open to understanding experiences outside of their own. Not all children arrive at school with ample exposure to or experience with empathy, but fortunately it can be taught. With instruction, modeling, practice, and meaningful application, students can internalize empathetic thinking, which, if repeated often enough, leads to its development as a habit.

Exploring perspective, inquiry, questioning, curiosity, respect, and analyzing experiences of a character are emphasized in this chapter through snapshots from different classrooms. A goal in the lessons highlighted in this chapter is to help students consider experiences and perspectives of others through literature, leading to a deeper understanding of—and appreciation for—diversity. Each teacher highlighted here selected their own text to ground a conversation with students.

YOUNG CHANGEMAKERS: FIRST GRADE WITH SARA

First-grade teacher Sara strives to make conversations about identity and empathy a daily practice in her first-grade classroom. Leveraging picture books and students' own experiences, Sara invites us in to observe how her students think about empathizing with others who are different, and what they might do to help everyone feel included. She chooses to read *Amy Wu and the Warm Welcome* by Kat Zhang.[7]

Upon introducing and starting the story, which features a character (Lin) who has recently immigrated to the United States and isn't speaking in class, students begin to make inferences about how the character Lin might feel. A first student observes that Lin probably feels "shy and nervous," with another chiming in that "he looks afraid." Sara nudges the students to consider why Lin's character might appear this way, and they share insights such as: "He might feel different from the other kids," and "He speaks a different language and he might be worried that they won't understand him." Students then begin to notice how the other character (Amy) appears, sharing that "They [Amy and Lin] speak different languages. She might be worried that Lin would laugh at her."

Sara takes this opportunity to connect the student insights to their own lives, helping to bridge the gap between fictional characters and their own experiences. She poses the question: "I'm hearing several of you mention language. Do you know anyone who speaks a different language from you?" Most students nod their heads.

Pause & Reflect: How can you connect what students see/hear in a picture book to their own experiences inside and outside of school?

A teacher's intentional decisions around the types of questions and the amount of processing time make a huge difference in the level of understanding gleaned from a read-aloud and discussion. In this example, Sara takes the time to intentionally provide wait time for students to process and reflect about the prompts she posed, which leads to deeper understanding.

The book comes to a close with Sara integrating various pause points for students to process; students share what actions Amy took to help make the new character Lin feel welcome. Students share their observations that Amy played with him and accepted him despite their differences. Sara then asks students to consider what the author's message in this story might be (determining the central message of a story is a key Common Core Standard). Several students share their learning about empathy, with comments such as: "It's okay for people to be different and speak different languages," and "To teach people not to laugh at others . . . we shouldn't laugh at others if they are nervous, different, or if they make a mistake." A third student speaks up with something very insightful: "People talk in different languages but they are like us too," which addresses the notion that while people have different identity markers, we are often more similar than different. Had Sara's students not come to this observation on their own, she might have specifically asked how the characters were similar despite language differences.

A final student demonstrates a complex understanding of identity by sharing that the author's message is "to tell people it's [they're] allowed to feel nervous and shy about meeting people who are different from you." Here, the student also demonstrates empathy for Amy, who ends up befriending the new student Lin. This is critical, as it validates the real feelings that many students share when encountering difference, while affirming connection over division. Sara affirms that this often takes bravery, but is an important part of building community. Sara's discussions take the stance that "care and love are the foundations of critical work," which invites students to advocate for critical changes through the lens of empathy for others.[8]

Sara then connects this lesson to character traits that students have been learning—specifically curiosity. She poses an interesting question: "We've been reflecting and learning about the characteristic of curiosity. How might curiosity help someone new feel more welcome?" In doing so, Sara addresses the Learning for Justice Diversity Anchor Standard 8: "Students will respectfully express curiosity about the history and lived experiences of others and will exchange ideas and beliefs in an open-minded way."[9] She stresses that an attitude of curiosity toward new people and experiences can help build bridges between others. Students respond with statements such as: "If you're curious, you can ask questions about their lives and be friends with them," "If you ask someone new some questions, I think they might feel special," and finally, "If you're new, and other kids ask you questions, you feel like they care about you," indicating that asking questions is a great way to begin a friendship. Sara affirms all of these responses, agreeing that asking questions about someone's life is a way to show care.

To bring this conversation back to how students can create tangible impact within their community and world, Sara asks them to think about steps that they can take to make the world a better place. Most students share instances of kindness, respect, helping others, and doing activities with other people. A student shares an observation, then, that "we cannot segregate," and Sara asks the student to elaborate. The student continues: "We can't put people in different places, we should all get along. White and Black people should be able to be in the same places." Importantly, this young student is connecting the very real social issue of racism to improving the world and the lives of other people. Furthermore, this student believes that they have the agency to create real change in the

---

Pause & Reflect: How would you respond to this student's comment? Would you choose to unpack this connection? Why or why not?

Action Item: The next time you facilitate a conversation around identity or empathy, notice your response to uncomfortable silence from students. Do you tend to step and rescue students from engaging in the conversation? Or do you let them productively struggle forward?

world—something Sara strives for when having these types of discussions with her class.

This opens up opportunities for other students to show specific actions that can make the world better. Students share insights such as: "Another thing to make the world better is to keep the earth clean. Keep the planet safe," "Giving compliments to other people," and "Helping others, learning to be friends, and not hating each other." A final student shares a perceptive comment: "We can be role models." Sara asks this student to elaborate on what they mean by role model, and the student explains that it can be showing other people what kindness looks like. Even as some of our youngest learners, Sara's students demonstrate a level of complexity in their thinking, but also the confidence that they can influence the actions of other people.

As this lesson comes to a close, Sara emphasizes the wonderful ideas that students contributed, and conveys to students that she believes they have a lot of knowledge to share on this topic. The first graders highlighted here have received many messages that their ideas matter and that they can create a positive change in the world.

Pause & Reflect: How can you emphasize to students that you believe in their capacity to make a difference in the world?

INTERMEDIATE STUDENTS EXPLORE THE THEME OF EMPATHY: FOURTH GRADE WITH ANNIE

The Other Side by Jacqueline Woodson is the text that Annie chooses for her lesson on theme.[10] She correctly predicted that the level of enthusiasm for this particular text would be high among her students due to the relevancy of the topic and their own lived experiences in their diverse community.

As Annie begins the story, she asks students to share their initial thoughts, which include: "It was racist that the White girl and the Black girl couldn't play together," and "It shouldn't matter what color your skin is." One student comments on the fact that the White girl in the story came down from the fence to play with the Black girl in her yard, but not the other way around. He infers it could have been that the Black girl was too afraid to go over to the White girl's yard, and that it wasn't fair.

Annie next poses the question: "When the girls in the story said that *someday, someone will knock this fence down,* what did that mean?" One student shares she thinks it means that people of different colors of skin will eventually become equal. Another comments, "If I was the author of this story, I'd change the ending so that the grown-ups said, 'You can go on both sides of the fence from now on.'" Annie chooses this teachable moment to introduce the literary device of metaphor, followed by asking what they think the fence is a metaphor for. The first student to comment answers that it is a metaphor for segregation. Another student feels it is a metaphor for bias and hate. Students begin to generate multiple questions at that point, such as: "I wonder who made the fence?," "How long was the fence and did it go all through the town or was it just between those two houses?," and "Why did they build the fence in the first place?" As students feel comfortable posing questions for the class, it is easy to see that a culture of inquiry and shared ownership for learning has been established.

Annie shifts the conversation to the concept of theme (a key Common Core Standard in fourth grade), and students recall that theme means the heart of a story, and can be a moral or message.[11] They share a wealth of ideas for the theme of this story. Some of their ideas include:

"No matter what skin color, people are all human."

"Forbidden friends decided to be friends."

"Don't judge a book by its cover, and don't judge people by the color of their skin."

"People can be friends with people who are different from them."

"We should be anti-racist."

These fourth graders demonstrate comprehension of the complex skill of determining theme while having a challenging conversation about race. Rather than focusing on difference, students typically focus on the ways in which the characters in the text are similar, and how difference shouldn't preclude people from forming relationships. In doing so, the students demonstrate understanding of the Learning for Justice Diversity Anchor Standard 9: "Students will respond to diversity by building empathy, respect, understanding and connection."[12] In addition, Annie's skilled facilitation along with the culture of shared learning in the classroom allows students to have confidence that their thoughts and ideas are valued.

Pause & Reflect: In what ways have you established structures or provided practice that communicates that all voices in the classroom are important? Do students ask questions of one another? Do they have a sense of ownership in their own learning?

LEARNING ABOUT IMMIGRATION: FIFTH GRADE WITH LISA

Lisa's choice of *Areli Is a Dreamer* by Areli Morales for her lesson gives students an introduction to the Deferred Action for Childhood Arrivals (DACA) immigration policy through the experiences and words of the author, who traveled from Mexico to New York at the age of six.[13] This selection is intentional on Lisa's part, as she wants students to consider a perspective and background that differs from many of their own. An important note about Lisa's teaching practice is that she had the questions that she intended to ask identified prior to this lesson, and displays them on slides, which contribute to the engagement level of her students. Students are able to refer to the visuals throughout and the conversation can proceed without Lisa needing to restate the questions.

After Lisa introduces the title, she asks students to think about what they noticed about the front cover. She asks, "What connections are you making? What inferences can you make?" After giving ample wait time (which supports the students in formulating their thoughts), she prompts them to talk with their table groups about these questions. After bringing the class back to a whole-group discussion, one student notices the "true story" written on the cover. Another student notices a big city and what looks like a "hometown" on the cover, two different places. Lisa prompts students to consider what the two scenes on the front cover might have to do with the story. A first student responds that "maybe it's about the times of day, day and night." Another student shares that the city looks like New York City because he thinks some of the buildings look like ones he's seen there, and a third student adds on to that statement by predicting that the main character in the book moves to a big city.

Students continue the discussion, with a student noticing the word "dreamer" in the title and guessing that the book has something to do with creativity. Several students chime in to elaborate with: "Maybe she dreams of going to the city even though she lives in a smaller home town," and "She might want BIG things to happen, because if she dreams about it, it could come true." Another student shares: "I think she dreams of doing big things in a city." Lots of other students indicate that they agree with this statement.

Lisa then shares the author's note at the front of the book, which provides background information about the main character being an undocumented immigrant, how she is part of the Deferred Action for Childhood Arrivals (DACA) and how she has finally been able to come out of the shadows and pursue her dreams. Following the reading of the author's note, Lisa asks students what their thoughts are. A student offers: "Being an immigrant, Areli was new to this country and she didn't have anything and didn't know what to do. We have everything we need, but Areli doesn't."

Lisa begins the story, where Areli's family moves to New York City when she is still too young. Students begin to have a discussion around how Areli might feel, for example: "She might feel abandoned," "She might feel scared for [her brother] to go to a new place," and "She might be super nervous that [her brother] is making such a big change." Later in the story, when Areli is told by her *abuela* (grandmother) that she is also going to move to the United States, Lisa prompts students to consider how she might be feeling at this point. A first student shares that "she might be worried that her grandma might pass away and she might not see her again." Another student responds with: "The U.S. had better job opportunities, so she might be thinking it's best," although another student respectfully disagrees with this statement, sharing: "I'm not sure that the U.S. is better than Mexico."

Pause & Reflect: Would you unpack this last disagreement with your students? Where might these student insights come from (their own background, experience, or knowledge)?

The story continues, with Lisa pausing at various points to unpack the language and images in the text. For example, she pauses on a page where Areli begins her move (the illustration depicts Mexico on one side, and the U.S. on another), and students share insights based on the meaning behind the illustrations. A student comments: "It looks like all the changes Areli is experiencing because of the move," demonstrating how powerful the images in this text are at depicting the character's feelings around transition.

After reading the portion about the bullying Areli experienced when in the United States, and how one student said she was illegal, Lisa asks students to think to themselves about whether they think Areli should have to worry about being sent back to Mexico. She does not ask for verbal sharing at this point, though some students visibly share their feelings by shaking their heads no. In using literature, Lisa helps humanize the immigrant experience for her students through a lens that they can understand. This helps to work against dominant narratives of immigrants, especially those who come to the U.S. from Mexico, by having students empathize with the experience of a character who would be their peer. This, we believe, is the power of leveraging literature in these types of discussions.

At the conclusion of the story, several students audibly whisper, "Wow." Lisa shares that she notices that some of the students have emotions as they hear the story—some look angry, and some look like they feel empathy for Areli at some points, like when she was bullied. One student responds: "That girl went through a lot!" Another student comments: "It was a heavy story." A third adds: "It's like what lots of other people have gone through," demonstrating his knowledge of some shared experiences. The student reactions demonstrate the power of literature in giving us insight into the experiences of other people, which is critical for empathy. Lisa asks students to consider why Areli's parents wanted to move to the U.S., and students share reflections such as: "Maybe they could get better jobs," "Because they could get a better education, like college," "Their currency, their money might not have as much value," and "I think there might be more fighting and violence there." Not only do Lisa's students have empathy for Areli's immigration experience, but they also demonstrate empathy for Areli's family in seeking out opportunities.

Pause & Reflect: Lisa's classroom discussion points to the importance of being thoughtful in the literature used and deliberate in the questions posed. What are some of your own criteria when selecting books to share with your students?

Lisa then decides to connect the experience of Areli to experiences that her students may have had. She poses the question: "Have you ever moved to a new place, and if so, what do you remember about how you felt in a place where you didn't know anyone?" Lisa shares her own move from Oregon to Washington and feeling upset. However, after moving and meeting her second-grade teacher, she got a note from her teacher that said: "Welcome to our school." It made a big impression on Lisa as a child. She shares that she felt much calmer after getting that note from the teacher. Several students share similar sentiments about moving between states, with statements such as: "I've moved a lot and there were so many challenges, like learning how things are done in the new places."

A couple of students who have emigrated from other countries also share their experiences. A student responds: "Sometimes moving is a LONG trek. I moved from Ukraine," with another student with a similar experience adding on: "I went from Ukraine to California, then another place, then here. I felt scared because I didn't know anyone and didn't know English and I was worried because no one knew my language." A third student speaks up: "I moved here from China, and didn't know anyone, didn't know the language, didn't know the school. It was scary for me," and a final student adds: "I moved here from India and I don't remember much about India now, but it was hard at first." In allowing the space for students to share their own experience, Lisa not only creates a sense of empathy for Areli and one another, but she also invites students to know they're not alone in their experience. Inviting students to connect with characters and bring their own lived experience into the conversation will also strengthen the bonds within your classroom community.[14]

To expand the conversation, Lisa next asks students what helped make their school experience better, and furthermore, what all students can do to help newcomers feel a sense of belonging at school. This not only creates more space to share their own lives, but also leads into actions that they can take to create a sense of community for others. Students brainstorm ideas such as: "Students can invite new kids to play at recess," "Be friends with them," "We could ask what their skills or abilities are, like what sports they like," and "Sit with them at lunch." A final student comments: "Sometimes it just takes a smile," a poignant observation that a smile can cross barriers. Lisa validates all the comments, saying, "Yes, I've seen many of you listen to our new students from Ukraine; you've asked them about their worlds, and you've gotten to know them. Although they came from a land very far away, you do have lots of things in common, no matter where you come from. So listening to others helps us get to know them."

To close the discussion, Lisa asks students to consider the author's purpose for writing this story, one of the Common Core State Standards, prompting the students to dig deeply into the meaning of the story and the importance of the author's message about empathy and belonging.[15] Several students stay close to the immigration theme, stating that: "I think she wrote it so we could understand how immigrants might feel," "So that other immigrants know they are not alone," and finally, "I think she wanted to teach us about immigration." Other students take a broader approach, for example, with the comment: "She wants us to connect to another person's life, or another person's story." This student yet again demonstrates the power of literature in bringing people together, and through different perspective taking.

Although this particular read-aloud does not focus on advocacy, you can see that some students instinctively consider what they can do to support others and foster a sense of community, moving toward the Learning for Justice Action Anchor Standard 17: "Students will recognize their own responsibility to stand up to exclusion, prejudice and injustice."[16] Students close the discussion by saying: "The author wants us to dream big and to welcome people to our country," "We are all humans; it doesn't matter where you're from," and "We have a lot in common with people even if they've come from other places, and we need to be kind to everyone and help them feel like they belong." Importantly, due to Lisa's regular attention to books that lead to discussions about diversity and inclusion, her students are comfortable and adept at having this conversation about belonging, immigration, and perspectives.

Pause & Reflect: What types of questions lead to deeper discussions? Why is asking about the author's purpose so critical? What goals in using questioning strategies do you have?

When examining Sara's primary example all the way to Lisa's fifth-grade example, it becomes clear how, when these conversations are part of the classroom culture from an early age, students are able to empathize deeply with characters in literature. Gholdy Muhammad reminds us that when we learn about the cultures of other people, we learn to live in harmony with those who see the world differently.[17] Weaving character experiences with students' own background and experience provides a rich foundation for students to take on different perspectives, connect with one another, and build a stronger community. As in other chapters, these individual classroom lessons are not isolated events, but are part of the teachers' larger commitment to discussing identity and empathy with their students.

SUMMARY OF KEY POINTS FROM THIS CHAPTER

- Empathy is a skill that can be taught.
- Empathy can strengthen relationships, resolve conflicts, and help students understand the experiences of others.

- Discussions around literature can help students connect with others.
- Using "window" texts can provide multiple narratives for students.

SUGGESTED PICTURE BOOK LIST: KNOWLEDGE, PERSPECTIVE, AND EMPATHY: UNDERSTANDING OTHERS

Note: The suggested books for chapters 2 and 3 can be interchangeable, as what is a mirror for one child might be a window for another.

- *A Boy and a Jaguar* by Alan Rabinowitz (2014)
- *A Day with No Words* by Tiffany Hammond (2023)
- *All My Stripes: A Story for Children with Autism* by Shaina Rudolph (2015)
- *All People Are Beautiful* by Vincent Kelly (2021)
- *Amy Wu and the Warm Welcome* by Kat Zhang (2022)
- *Areli Is a Dreamer* by Areli Morales (2021)
- *Chocolate Milk Por Favor* by Maria Dismondy (2015)
- *Dancing Hands: How Teresa Carreño Played the Piano for President Lincoln* by Margarita Engle (2019)
- *Digging for Words: José Alberto Gutiérrez and the Library He Built* by Angela Burke Kunkel (2020)
- *Each Kindness* by Jacqueline Woodson (2012)
- *Fry Bread: A Native American Family Story* by Kevin Noble Maillard (2019)
- *Hair Love* by Matthle A. Cherry (2019)
- *I Talk Like a River* by Jordan Scott (2020)
- *Josie Dances* by Denise Lajimodiere (2021)
- *Just Ask! Be Different, Be Brave, Be You* by Sonia Sotomayor (2019)
- *Last Stop on Market Street* by Matt de la Pena (2015)
- *My Brother Is Away* by Sara Greenwood (2022)
- *Namaste Is a Greeting* by Suma Subramaniam (2022)
- *Our Diversity Makes Us Stronger* by Elizabeth Cole (2021)
- *Outside Amelia's Window* by Caroline Nastro (2023)
- *Room for Everyone* by Naaz Khan (2021)
- *Soon, Your Hands* by Jonathan Stutzman (2023)
- *Stacey's Remarkable Books* by Stacey Abrams (2022)
- *The 1619 Project: Born on the Water* by Nikole Hannah-Jones (2021)
- *The Bright Side* by Chad Otis (2023)
- *The Invisible* by Tom Percival (2021)
- *The Notebook Keeper: A Story of Kindness from the Border* by Stephen Briseno (2022)

- *The Other Side* by Jacqueline Woodson (2001)
- *The Skin You Live In* by Michael Tyler (2005)
- *Under My Hijab* by Hena Khan (2019)
- *We Are All Connected* by Gabi Barcia (2022)
- *We Can Do It* by Dawn McCuin (2021)
- *Where Butterflies Fill the Sky* by Zahra Marwan (2022)

NOTES

1. Costa, A., & Kallick, B. (2009). *Habits of mind across the curriculum*, p. 218. Alexandria, VA: Association for Supervision and Curriculum Development.
2. Adichie, C. (2009). *The danger of a single story* [Video]. TEDGlobal Conferences. Retrieved from https://www.ted.com/talks/chimamanda_ngozi_adichie_the_danger_of_a_single_story/
3. Kunkel, A. (2020). *Digging for words: Jose Alberto Gutierrez and the library he built*. New York: Schwartz & Wade Books.
4. Hannah-Jones, N., & Watson, R. (2021). *The 1619 Project: Born on the water*. New York: Penguin Random House.
5. Institute for the Habits of Mind. (2022). Retrieved from https://www.habitsofmindinstitute.org
6. Costa, A., & Kallick, B. (2009). *Habits of mind across the curriculum*. Alexandria, VA: Association for Supervision and Curriculum Development.
7. Zhang, K. (2022). *Amy Wu and the warm welcome*. New York: Simon & Schuster.
8. Campano, G., Ghiso, M. P., & Welch, B. J. (2016). *Partnering with immigrant communities: Action through literacy*. New York: Teachers College Press.
9. Southern Poverty Law Center (2021). *Frameworks*. Learning for Justice. Retrieved from https://www.learningforjustice.org/frameworks
10. Woodson, J. (2001). *The other side*. New York: Penguin Random House.
11. National Governors Association. (2010). Common Core State Standards. Washington, DC.
12. Southern Poverty Law Center (2021). *Frameworks*. Learning for Justice. Retrieved from https://www.learningforjustice.org/frameworks
13. Morales, A. (2021). *Areli is a dreamer: A true story by Areli Morales, a DACA recipient*. New York: Random House.
14. Esteban-Guitart, M., & Moll, L. C. (2014). Lived experience, funds of identity and education. *Culture & Psychology*, 20(1), 70–81.
15. National Governors Association. (2010). *Common Core State Standards*. Washington, DC: National Governors Association.
16. Southern Poverty Law Center (2021). *Frameworks*. Learning for Justice. Retrieved from https://www.learningforjustice.org/frameworks
17. Muhammad, G. (2020). *Cultivating genius: An equity framework for culturally and historically responsive literacy*. New York: Scholastic.

4

Advocacy and Action

Now What?

You may find that making a difference for others makes the biggest difference in you.—Brian Williams[1]

The snapshots presented in this section of the book ask students to synthesize their own understanding of their identity, their knowledge of other experiences, and their ability to take on different perspectives to advocate for change in the *world*, whether this is in their local community or a broader context. Simply, the goal of this chapter is to have students reflect on what they, as children, can do to make an impact on others through local civic action, the arts, public speaking, service to others, or in other meaningful ways.[2] Many of the picture books highlighted in this chapter identify real changemakers and provide examples of how advocates have created a tangible impact, and each teacher leads students through a conversation about their own role in making the world a better and more inclusive place. As you read these examples, reflect on your own learners and how you might structure discussions to encourage them to speak up for change about issues that they care about.

UNDERSTANDING HOW ANYONE CAN MAKE A DIFFERENCE: FOURTH GRADE WITH WENDY

In one fourth-grade classroom, for example, students discuss the themes in *Change Sings* and unpack what inclusion actually means.[3] With the academic goal of determining the author's message, Wendy begins by asking students to infer what the book is about. The story is a beautifully illustrated, lyrical poem by Amanda Gorman, focused on the many ways that each of us can make a change in our world. Therefore, as students determine Amanda Gorman's message, they are also learning and unpacking the ways that they might create change in their community through the examples in the book.

As Wendy asks students to make inferences about the book, responses include: "It's about someone who sings or plays music," "It might be an African American girl who might change music for girls," and "I think it's about an African American girl who makes songs." She asks students to share the evidence they used to make their inferences, integrating rigorous academic work while simultaneously affirming diversity and identities.

Because the book is written in poem form, Wendy next asks students to pay attention to how the text and the images interact, because the illustrations are purposeful and part of the author's message. In this lesson, Wendy draws from the Common Core State Standards for fourth grade (Reading Standard 2: Determine theme of a story; Reading Standard 7: Make connections between the text of a story and a visual presentation of the text).[4] However, because Wendy also asks students to point out concrete actions that they observe as they listen to the story, she also touches on the Learning for Justice Standards—in particular, Action Anchor Standard 16: "Students will express empathy when people are excluded or mistreated because of their identities and concern when they themselves experience bias."[5] As you will see, these separate sets of standards come together in this lesson to help students deeply understand a text while relating it to their own lives and community. When planning for discussions with your students, we encourage you to consider integrating academic content standards with social justice standards—these objectives need not be separate.

On one particular page, Dr. Martin Luther King Jr. is portrayed, and Wendy asks students what they notice in the illustration. Students recognize who it is in the illustration, but Wendy probes even further to ask: "Why do you think the author wanted his picture here?" Several students respond with similar sentiments: "To make a connection to MLK's famous speech," "She's [Amanda Gorman] trying to make change in the world, like MLK," "She's trying to be like him," and finally, "Maybe he's her idol." In doing so, students astutely infer that Amanda Gorman uses the illustration of Dr. Martin Luther King Jr. to draw connections between his famous quest for justice and the everyday acts of change that are portrayed throughout the story.

Wendy asks students to unpack some of what they are seeing and learning as they progress through the book. One student states: "I notice that the setting is now in a park. I see the boy is now helping to clean up the park." Many students signal their agreement with this statement. A second adds on: "I think she's [Amanda Gorman] changing his mind, to change the planet, to clean up this world. She's being a role model."

Another student synthesizes these comments with an insightful statement: "It's a tiny little dot, like one person, trying to change the world." Here, students make the connection that even one individual can make change and set an example for others. Shortly after, another student builds on this comment: "I notice Amanda, since she's a poet and they have instruments, she's using poetry to make change," which also brings to light that there are many different ways that individuals can effect change.

A focus on student activism often discusses adolescents.[6] We argue that the stage for youth participation can be set in early grades, where students feel that their voices are recognized and are therefore compelled to amplify them. Furthermore, this brings teachers and students together and builds trust while cultivating a sense that students can also be leaders.

Pause & Reflect: How might you engage students in brainstorming to see the many different ways that individuals can create change in their community?

Connecting the Text to Student Lives

As the class discussion nears the end of the book and students have discussed multiple examples of creating change, Wendy turns their attention also to the images of the text in order to dig deeper into the symbolism that the images represent (addressing Common Core Standard for Reading 7, fourth grade). One student shares their understanding of the bridges and fences in the book: "Fences separate people. Bridges bring them together," and another adds on: "I see a person in a wheelchair. They're making a ramp. They're helping the person by building a ramp." They connect overt acts such as building a wheelchair ramp so that people with disabilities can access the same places as everyone else, to language of inclusion and the desire to help others with examples such as: "The person can now go down the ramp! He can be included."

Finally, another student shares: "Every time I see someone being nice, it's like MLK Jr. What MLK Jr. symbolized is about making change for people that couldn't be together. Like if it was a fence, the kids are making a bridge to connect people like MLK was trying to do." The students demonstrate their ability to make connections between historical figures and events and their present-day lives because Wendy helps facilitate these connections with her line of questioning. For example, in asking students to articulate the deeper meanings of the bridge and fence in this text, Wendy pushes their thinking beyond the surface to reach the lesson's academic objective (determining the author's message). This connection that her students make is crucial for supporting students in developing agency and envisioning actions that they can take, whether that might be through civic action, service acts, art forms, or in other ways.

Wendy closes this discussion by returning to the lesson objective of determining the author's message in the story. Students share insights such as: "I think she's saying as you make changes, they grow as well, more people join in," "Like one little thing can make a big difference," and finally, "When the title says *Change Sings*, by singing it goes across the world! We all want to be part of it." Because Wendy has clear goals for this session and yet keeps the conversation fluid and responsive to student observations, she is able to successfully author a "living curriculum" where student contributions have an active role in shaping the learning.[7] This parallels one key tenet of culturally responsive pedagogy, which is to believe in the intellect of students, and to structure teaching so that students can shine.[8]

In talking with Wendy after this lesson, we learned that this type of book, which highlighted diversity, inclusion, and advocacy, was not an anomaly for her to share with her class. Wendy, in her desire to position students who would feel empowered to make the world a better, more empathetic place, frequently engages in similar discussions with her students. Therefore, it isn't this one singular discussion that will create the largest impact, it is instead a series of similar discussions that will help students see themselves as leaders. Wendy is optimistic that these students will do just that—go out and change the world for the better.

Pause & Reflect: How might you have similar conversations with students that could empower them to make a difference in the world?

UNDERSTANDING CHANGEMAKERS WITH RUBY BRIDGES: THIRD GRADE WITH KATIE

The students in the previous example, in their reflections of advocacy, picked up on the symbolism throughout the story. Next, we highlight a third-grade example to demonstrate how slightly younger elementary students have clear thoughts about how they can make a positive impact in their community.

Katie opted to read *I Am Ruby Bridges* as part of ongoing discussions and celebrating Black History Month.[9] As you will see, however, she extends this conversation beyond a historical event and helps students make clear connections to their own lives. This is a key component of multicultural education, which argues that topics such as racism shouldn't be taught as solely an issue of the past but, rather, integrated into content and made relevant to students.[10] Katie brings the historical event of Ruby Bridges attending an all-White school to the foreground by connecting it to what students see—and experience—today.

Before starting the story, students immediately begin making connections and predicting the topic of the story, key practices that Katie integrates into her daily teaching. One student predicts that "it shows how Black and White people can be friends," likely drawing on prior knowledge of who Ruby Bridges is. A second student shares: "It's a true story." While this may seem obvious, this student also helps set the stage for a much deeper conversation—to help his peers understand that accounts of unfairness and injustice are not only things you learn about in school, but that also occur in the broader world. While Katie holds this discussion in the community of her classroom, what the students will learn have much wider-reaching implications.

As Katie reads the story, she draws student attention to an illustration of a bridge, where Ruby says she will bridge a gap between Black and White people. She asks students to subsequently think about how Ruby is bridging a gap between her actions and telling her story.

A student observes: "The laws got changed and Ruby showed how people of different skin colors could go to school together," and another student adds to that comment by sharing: "She was the first Black kid in a White school. She showed that kids of different colors could get along together." A third student shares here that "it shows that no matter what color your skin is, everyone should be respected."

Katie then asks students to think about their communities today, and whether it is important for people to try to "bridge gaps"—in other words, to advocate for change. Some of the students continue to discuss the events in *I Am Ruby Bridges* through a historical lens. For example, one student shares: "Yes [it's important to bridge gaps], because before, when Black and White people were separated, it wasn't good. It wasn't fair." Another student agrees: "I think it's an important lesson from history." With this comment, however, the student begins to suggest that while this event happened years ago, there is still much to learn.

In this pause in the story, a third student shares why he believes it's important to bridge gaps: "Because we need people to get along, be nice to each other. It was a sad time in history and we don't want that to happen again." Katie's students are thinking deeply about the story, and though some are not yet making connections to our present-day society, these conversations lay important foundations in order for them to do so.

However, another student boldly asserts: "Some people today still want segregation. It's not right," demonstrating her connection from the historical context of the story to the racial inequities that persist today. A different student shares a similar connection: "I know of a building manager that made someone move out of the building and it wasn't fair." This connection is especially poignant, as the student connects racial discrimination with income discrimination and the inequities that persist within social classes, taking a verbal stand. While potentially not even realizing it, this student makes important observations about privilege, and the ways in which our identity markers (such as race and socioeconomic status) intersect.

By voicing that "it wasn't fair," this student also takes a critical eye to complex social issues—particularly those less talked about in schools—such as housing. As Stephanie Jones argues, these types of discussions can "open up spaces where students can claim value in their experiences and critique mainstream ideals that marginalize them and their families."[11] By allowing students to make these connections, they are able to integrate their personal experiences and knowledge of the real world with literature, building a foundation for critical literacy.

Pause & Reflect: How might you help your own students make connections between historical events/injustice to their present-day world?

The power of having literature-based discussions, such as this one, with the entire class is that students are learning from the observations, insights, and beliefs of their fellow classmates. Through the probing questions of the teacher, and insights of their classmates, students are addressing the Learning for Justice Action Anchor Standard 17: "Students will recognize their own responsibility to stand up to exclusion, prejudice and injustice."[12] Katie firmly believes that her students of all backgrounds and identities have a lot to say, following in Gholdy Muhammad's encouragement to believe in the brilliance of each of our students.[13] In doing so, Katie carves out the space for them to share their insights, and this is where the richness in conversation happens.

Wanting to help students make further connections to their own lives and see themselves as changemakers, Katie asks students to reflect on how they can make positive changes in the world. Some students share how they can be good and kind friends to others. Others desire to make a change by teaching and being an example to others: "We can help people to learn that all people are good. Teach the people to do the right things." Finally, a student states: "I could make a community where people go to meet others and teach them how to make it better. Those people could reach out to other people. So good things could spread." By highlighting the example of Ruby Bridges, students begin to see that they can also be catalysts for change.

The last student comment during this discussion is: "We should be able to go to any school, like we do now. That shouldn't change." As this student demonstrates, students are seeing a historical moment and connecting it with present-day injustices. This plants a seed for students to speak up about injustices that they do see in their lives and the lives of others.

Like in the first example shared with Wendy, the third-grade snapshot here is not an isolated conversation. Students have heard many other diverse texts, and are equipped to share their observations and understandings as they hear a read-aloud. While celebrating Black History Month by reading diverse texts is a start, deeper learning and a sense of belonging is achieved only when this is a consistent part of classroom practice within a safe, inclusive class culture.

ADVOCACY AMONG OUR YOUNGEST STUDENTS: KINDERGARTEN WITH KRISTI

Through the Lebron James book *I Promise*, kindergarten students learn how young people make vows to improve their lives, achieve goals, help one another, and stand up for what they believe is right.[14] As this lesson begins, Kristi asks her kindergarten students to share their understanding of the word "promise." Responses include: "It means I will say I'm sorry if I've hurt someone," and "A promise could be that you'll keep a secret." Finally, "A promise can be something you say you will do to make the world better." This student seems to understand that a promise is akin to setting a goal, and ties it specifically to making a difference in our world.

Upon beginning the story, Kristi comments that she notices that the illustrator uses pictures of children with different skin colors, and one student chimes in: "That's because children *do* have different colors of skin!" Another follows with: "You're born with different colors of skin."

One student shares that she likes the story because the teacher wears a hijab like hers. Kristi's reply, modeling diversity as a strength, is: "Yes, we've talked about that a lot, and yes, we are all different, and isn't that a good thing? Each of you is unique. It doesn't matter if you have different hair colors, different colors of skin, or different clothes because we are all unique and special."

Kristi teaches respect and advocacy for all people with the statement: "In this book we learned about promises that children can make to take care of ourselves, be our best selves, and to stand up for what is right. What is a promise you could make to yourself?" Students share the following responses: "I will never, ever, share a secret," "I promise to be brave," "I promise to never give up, like in soccer I will keep trying and practicing," "I promise to be nice to other people," "I think being nice makes the world better," and finally, "I think being kind to people who are different is a good thing."

As this classroom snapshot illustrates, even very young children can demonstrate empathy and advocate for the value of diversity. They show compassion and the desire to make a positive difference in their relationships, schools, and communities. Our world could learn a lot from hearing the responses of Kristi's kindergarten students.

Pause & Reflect: In what other ways could you reinforce the students' convictions to make the world a better place?

MY VOICE IS A TRUMPET: FOURTH GRADE WITH LEILA

Leila begins the story *My Voice Is a Trumpet* by asking students to infer what the title might mean, a common practice when facilitating an interactive read-aloud.[15] A student shares: "That people's voices can be heard" while another student adds on: "That my voice can be heard even if some people can't hear me." These statements demonstrate that the students understand that the notion of having a voice, and speaking up, is not literal in this context. In priming students with this question, Leila sets the stage for students to consider how the individuals in the story stand up for what they believe is right. This lyrical picture book celebrates the many different kinds of voices (e.g., whether soft or loud), arguing that all are equally important and everyone has the capacity to use their voice for change.

Leila begins the read-aloud and comes to a section of the text that states: "We're sisters and brothers"; she asks students to consider what the author might mean by this statement. A student aptly responds: "I think he means that we should work together like some families do, working for good things to happen." Equality and inclusion are themes that students also pick up on, even when not directly stated: "Everyone is important. Everyone's voice is important and should be heard." As students begin to share these insights, Leila draws their attention more specifically to pinpointing the text's theme based on the details in the text—a key literacy standard in fourth grade.[16]

An important part of this text is the visual racial diversity that is portrayed throughout, and Leila wants to draw students' attention to this deliberate choice. Students agree that this choice is important to the overall message with statements such as: "Yes [it is important], because he wanted to show that people who are different can all have a voice and can all get along," and "It was important because there is a lot of racism and we need to work together to stop it." Importantly, this last student uses the present tense to talk about racism and the persistent nature of it, just as Katie's third-grade students did in a previous snapshot. In addition, students hint at the need to collaborate and work as a community to make positive change in the world.

A student builds on this part of the discussion with: "He [the author] was showing that everyone, people from different races, all have a voice and should use it." This statement, in particular, is a call to action from this student, who recognizes that issues such as racism and racial discrimination are issues that belong to everyone, and that everyone must play a part in dismantling them. A final student shares an insight: "People need to work together to fight racism, to show respect for everyone no matter what the color of their skin." Using your own voice—in whatever manner that means to you—to stand up for what is right is a pivotal value to students. This aligns with the Learning for Justice Action Anchor Standards, which ask students to identify *how* they will take a stand, rather than assuming that there is one correct way to do so.[17]

Pause & Reflect: How might you help students understand that there are many different ways to speak up?

Because the intent of this read-aloud is to also help students reflect on ways that they can be changemakers, the final component of this discussion asks students to reflect. Students share a wide spectrum of reflections, showing that they care about their communities, but each student foregrounds the issues that matter the most to them.

Some of the fourth graders focus on how to show and spread kindness. For example, several students share responses such as: "We can use our voices to ask people to be kind to people who are different from them," and "I can talk with people about being kind." Leila accepts all answers here, understanding and affirming that students can make a positive change in many different degrees.

Several students focus on a specific issue: "I will use my voice to teach people not to judge by gender," with another sharing: "I can use my voice to speak up against bullying. And to get people to wear masks to stop COVID-19. And to stop bad chemicals from spreading in the world." Students demonstrate through these statements that they are passionate about a variety of social issues, both locally and globally. In addition, this last student demonstrates a trajectory of influence, beginning with the impact on one person (bullying) and moving toward the impact on a larger community (chemicals).

Of course, many students also name racism directly, which the book subtly highlights. Students share insights such as: "I can teach people about racism and that it should stop," and "I can make posters to put up in neighborhoods. We need people to use kind words. Even kids can sometimes stop bullying and hate. Bullying can be a type of racism." This last student stands firm in the belief that "even kids" have the power to influence the actions of adults.

Pause & Reflect: How would you affirm these student observations and responses?

Key in these statements is that the students position themselves as having agency. This is contrasted with the more traditional view that adults hold knowledge and children learn from that adult knowledge. This can be even further contrasted with Paulo Freire's "banking" model of education, one where teachers teach and students absorb information.[18] In articulating the ways in which they can actively shape their community, students take ownership over their learning, as well as the kind of world that they want to live in.

Finally, a student shares that "I can be part of a peaceful protest; sometimes that is how change happens," sharing knowledge that protests have been part of civil rights historically, but also more recently and visibly. Also addressing current racial violence, a final student asserts: "I can use my voice to talk with my friends and other people about showing respect for Black people. Too many Black people are being killed."

These final statements highlight a conviction that many students share in addressing—and stopping—issues such as racial violence that have become so visible in our daily lives. Furthermore, we can infer that this student understands that we should all contribute to dismantling racism through conversation and understanding.

In the conclusion of this read-aloud and discussion, students begin to articulate specific actions that they will take to advocate for change, through teaching, protesting, and creating visuals. The more general phrases highlighted throughout the text suddenly become very real for students, as they grapple with how to stand up to injustice.

While we should not assume that every student in this discussion has a personal commitment to standing up for injustice, some students do begin to address the Learning for Justice Action Anchor Standard 19: "Students will make principled decisions about when and how to take a stand against bias and injustice in their everyday lives and will do so despite negative peer or group pressure."[19]

Pause & Reflect: In a classroom discussion like this, how might even more students be encouraged to articulate how they could use their voices to further the social justice issues they care about?

As you can see through these snapshots, students are in a variety of stages in terms of articulating their own personal feelings about advocacy. Each teacher highlighted here gives students examples of changemakers through texts (and in this case, we invite you to use all forms of text), and then asks students to connect it to their own lives. After all, this is where the meaning and rich conversation are.

While we have presented these classroom snapshots as just that—a moment in time—what is key is that they do not operate in isolation but are part of a broader context in the classroom presented. Each of these teachers expresses a commitment to discussing identity, empathy, and advocacy with their students on an ongoing basis, and the insights from students that you see on these pages have culminated from those ongoing discussions.

SUMMARY OF KEY POINTS FROM THIS CHAPTER

- Students of all ages can make an impact on their community in different ways.

- Students can make connections between history and present-day injustices.
- Encourage students to integrate their personal experiences and knowledge of the real world with literature.
- When facilitating, it's important to have clear goals for discussion, and yet remain responsive to student observations.

SUGGESTED PICTURE BOOK LIST: ADVOCACY AND ACTION

- *All the Way to the Top: One Girl's Fight for Americans with Disabilities* by Annette Bay Pimentel (2020)
- *Be a Friend* by Salina Yoon (2016)
- *Change Sings* by Amanda Gorman (2021)
- *Front Desk* by Kelly Yang (2018)
- *Harriet Tubman* by Ma Isabel Sanchez Vegara (2018)
- *Hey Wall: A Story of Art and Community* by Susan Verde (2018)
- *I Am Ruby Bridges* by Ruby Bridges (2022)
- *I Promise* by LeBron James (2020)
- *Just Help! How to Build a Better World* by Sonia Sotomayor (2022)
- *My Voice Is a Trumpet* by Jimmie Allen (2021)
- *Our Skin: A First Conversation about Race* by Megan Madison, Jessica Ralli, and Isabel Roxas (2021)
- *She Sang for India: How M. S. Subbulakshmi Used Her Voice for Change* by Suma Subramaniam (2022)
- *Stacey's Extraordinary Words* by Stacey Abrams (2021)
- *The People's Painter: How Ben Shahn Fought for Justice with Art* by Cynthia Levinson (2021)
- *We Are Together* by Britta Teckentrup (2022)

NOTES

1. Williams, B. (2023). Institute Success [Quote]. Retrieved from https://institutesuccess.com/library/you-may-find-that-making-a-difference-for-others-makes-the-biggest-difference-in-you-brian-williams/

2. Comber, B., Thomson, P., & Wells, M. (2001). Critical literacy finds a "place": Writing and social action in a low-income Australian grade 2/3 classroom. *Elementary School Journal, 101*(4), 451–464.

3. Gorman, A. (2021). *Change sings: A children's anthem.* New York: Viking.

4. National Governors Association. (2010). *Common Core State Standards.* Washington, DC: National Governors Association.

5. Southern Poverty Law Center (2021). *Frameworks*. Learning for Justice. Retrieved from https://www.learningforjustice.org/frameworks

6. Chang, E., & Gamez, R. (2022). Educational leadership as accompaniment: From managing to cultivating youth activism. *Teachers College Record, 124*(9), 65–90.

7. Genishi, C., & Dyson, A. H. (2009). *Children, language, and literacy: Diverse learners in diverse times*. New York: Teachers College Press.

8. Ladson-Billings, G. (2009). *The dreamkeepers*. San Francisco: Jossey-Bass.

9. Bridges, R. (2022). *I am Ruby Bridges*. New York: Scholastic.

10. Banks, J. A., & Banks, C. A. M. (Eds.). (2019). *Multicultural education: Issues and perspectives*. New York: Wiley.

11. Jones, S. (2006). *Girls, social class, and literacy: What teachers can do to make a difference*, p. 60. Portsmouth, NH: Heinemann.

12. Southern Poverty Law Center (2021). *Frameworks*. Learning for Justice. Retrieved from https://www.learningforjustice.org/frameworks

13. Muhammad, G. (2020). *Cultivating genius: An equity framework for culturally and historically responsive literacy*. New York: Scholastic.

14. James, L. (2020). *I promise*. New York: HarperCollins.

15. Allen, J. (2021). *My voice is a trumpet*. New York: Flamingo Books.

16. National Governors Association. (2010). *Common Core State Standards*. Washington, DC: National Governors Association.

17. Southern Poverty Law Center (2021). *Frameworks*. Learning for Justice. Retrieved from https://www.learningforjustice.org/frameworks

18. Freire, P. (1970). *Pedagogy of the oppressed*. London: Penguin.

19. Southern Poverty Law Center (2021). *Frameworks*. Learning for Justice. Retrieved from https://www.learningforjustice.org/frameworks

5

When Things Don't
Go as Planned

As you begin your own inside-out work in this area, your lizard brain will start to freak out. It's afraid that you will have to talk about sensitive issues such as race, racism, classism, sexism, or any other kind of "-ism." It is afraid that this conversation will make you vulnerable and open to some type of emotional or physical attack. But this fear is not real. It is just your amygdala's ploy to get you to stay in your comfort zone.—Zaretta L. Hammond[1]

Every educator experiences this . . . the unplanned comments, questions, or behaviors from students that are surprising, upsetting, or triggering. Most educators have also experienced concerns, pushback, accusations, or other challenges from caregivers, colleagues, or community members. Organized in sections focusing on students, colleagues, and parents/community members, this chapter will provide strategies to demonstrate how teachers and other educators have handled and addressed these situations. Guidance for crafting your *why* and proactively keeping lines of communication open will be explored.

CRAFTING YOUR *WHY*

Your *why* is your purpose, the cause, or the beliefs that inspire you to devote your time, energy, and passion to this work. Another way to think about it is your *why* is your anchor. The purpose of an anchor is to keep your vessel safely positioned so that you can retain your position and not be swept away. In terms of education, your *why* will sustain you in difficult times. In this kind of work, you will be challenged; you will experience pushback, heartache, and defeat. There will be times when you'll want to give up. But if you can remain tethered to your *why*, it can keep you grounded and help you sustain your energy to move forward to achieve your goals.

As you seek to inspire, teach, and lead others, they will want to understand why you are committed to this work. Reflect on turning points in your life and how they impacted you. Who have been the most influential people in your life so far? Consider your role models and what you learned from them. What are the events and experiences that have shaped you? For some people, their *why* comes from personal challenges they've faced. For others, it comes from learning about challenges of others and seeing injustices. It could also be that your *why* emerged from personal celebrations or successes of others. Take some time to ponder this, and be ready to articulate why you care deeply about this work.

Here is an activity that might be helpful in crafting your *why*. As you think about your life experiences, write down ten values you feel are pertinent to your work. Next, narrow your list by keeping just the five values most important to you. Finally, of those five values, which are the top one or two that you feel are most critical to being a successful educator? Where does equity or belonging fit into your list? Why do you think you feel passionate about it? Why do you believe it will change the world for the better? Try crafting a *why* paragraph. Write it down and, after a day or two, reread it to see if you want to revise it. Share it with trusted friends and ask for feedback to determine if it's clear. Does it resonate with you? Know that your *why* can be modified over time as you evolve as an individual and leader, but devote time to this important aspect of being a leader in this work. We can't emphasize this enough!

WHEN THINGS DON'T GO AS PLANNED WITH STUDENTS

Teachable Moments

Part of a classroom community that lends itself to critical conversations is using spontaneous student comments or questions as teachable moments, especially when the comments are misguided or lack contextual knowledge. Ignoring comments or questions may perpetuate misunderstanding for some students, and disregard the lived reality of others. It can also lead to serious long-term problems for affected students including anxiety and mental health challenges. Instead of ignoring misguided comments, getting curious about students and their perspectives can open up additional avenues for questioning and educating students about the intent and impact on others.

If a topic or question has captured a student's attention, and if the teacher thinks the topic or question is of interest to others in the class, it might be time well spent to take the opportunity to answer or explore the topic. Since teachable moments are unplanned, the teacher must feel comfortable in addressing the topic and in diverting from the lesson plan. However, the inherent interest sparked by a student's question or comment might justify the time and risk of proceeding without a prepared plan because of students' receptivity and increased capacity for learning.

Scenarios of Teachers Seizing on a Teachable Moment

In a third-grade class, a student said to an Asian classmate: "Your eyes are really small because you're Asian. You need glasses." Rather than limiting her response to reteaching kindness, the teacher's response was to lean in, inquire, and be curious. She asked, "Can you tell us why you think that?" After the student replied: "Her eyes are so narrow," the teacher added "Yes, we all have eyes that are different from one another. But smaller eyes don't mean a person needs glasses, and it was an unkind thing to say. We need to celebrate the ways in which we are alike and different from other people."

The teacher went on to dive deeper by introducing that sometimes people stereotype, or lump everyone in a specific race or gender as alike, adding that it is an example of a generalization. She pointed out that within those races or genders there are many differences. She continued to explain that stereotypes can be hurtful to others and that they would explore stereotypes more on another day.

A second example is in a fifth-grade class, a student said: "I don't like Black people." Another student replied: "Rashon [a biracial classmate] is Black, so that means you don't like Rashon."

The teacher's response was to address this teachable moment and be curious. She replied to the first student: "Tell us more. What do you mean?" The student stated: "I don't like him because Black people are always causing trouble." "What kind of trouble are you talking about?" asked the teacher. This gave the teacher an opportunity to learn more about the first student's perceptions, and she decided to say: "That's something we should talk about more. I'm going to do some research and make sure we return to this topic next week." In this case, the teacher wanted to consult with the school counselor and others in addition to doing research so that she could feel more prepared to have this conversation with her class.

We don't always have the answers, especially when concerns like these come up spontaneously. However, by this teacher assuring the class that they would return to the discussion, it communicated to students that it wouldn't be ignored. Give yourself permission to push pause in instances where you want to be more prepared; just make sure that you do return to the topic on another day, as promised. When students see that you are listening and following through, they will trust you and lines of communication will be kept open.

Pause & Reflect: Can you recall any teachable moments that weren't addressed in the moment? Are any of those events possible to still address even though time has passed?

Using Restorative Practices

Just as students are learning academic content and skills, they are also learning how to get along with others in and out of school. Mistakes will be made, and seeing misbehavior as opportunities to reteach sets students up for learning. It also communicates a growth mindset that we are all learners who can repair harm we've caused and rebuild relationships.

Our experiences with the National Center for Restorative Justice have been instrumental as we've introduced restorative practices in schools.[2] As opposed to punitive and traditional approaches to discipline, restorative practices promote building and maintaining healthy relationships, nurturing and respecting the inherent dignity and worth of each person, and aiming to support a sense of belonging for every student while nurturing intentional accountability and repair to those impacted and to the community.

While restorative justice in education is not limited to instances of misbehavior or conflict, it is an approach that can make a positive difference when conflict does occur. Conflict will happen, and when it does, having a focus on learning, repairing harm, and restoring relationships pays off in more ways than can be counted.

Scenario of Restorative Practices in First Grade

A first-grade teacher in a diverse school district uses daily classroom meetings to build relationships and connections, teach routines, and reinforce expectations. A talking piece is used, and the person holding the talking piece talks while others listen. For the talking piece, she uses a mason jar, which holds sticky notes that students have used to record their names and something they like. For the circle meetings, she uses the norms of:

- Sit in a circle.
- Use the talking piece.
- Listen carefully.
- Be kind and respectful.
- Be confidential.

She finds that the procedures used in the daily circles enable her to hold small-group accountability circles when conflict occurs. In those instances, there are up to six people who participate in the circle, and the goal is for students to understand the impact of their behaviors on others.

Scenario of Restorative Practices in Intermediate Grades

A fifth-grade teacher in the same school has been implementing restorative practices for several years. He feels passionate about using the first weeks of school to build relationships, teach empathy, and use daily, morning circles as one of their essential strategies. Their grade-level teams collaborate to create slides with questions/prompts that are used in each of the morning circles. During the first weeks as students are getting to know one another, they use the frame of: "Would you rather _____ or _____?" Given that many multilingual learners are in their classes, simple frames like this supported those students in participating.

Similar to the first-grade teacher, this teacher shared that students internalize expectations from the daily morning circles, which transfer to more difficult circles if and when something has gone wrong. Having this framework already in place allows the teacher to have restorative justice conversations in a format that students know. An example he shared with us was when he returned to school after an absence and learned that students had been very disrespectful to the substitute teacher. After having students do some personal reflection in writing, he facilitated a circle to process the day with the substitute teacher who was impacted about how they could take responsibility. One of the prompts he used in the circle was: "I want to be accountable for _____." As the talking piece went around the circle, each student shared their thoughts. We found it interesting that it wasn't limited to misbehavior—some students shared positive actions they had shown, such as: "I want to be accountable for trying to quiet other students down."

Another intermediate-grade teacher models the facilitation of morning circles for the first few months of school, then asks the students to articulate what they notice in terms of her facilitation. Their comments include: "You give positive reinforcement," "You use a prompt for everyone to respond to," and "You use the talking stick." Through the students' keen observations, they learn successful facilitation techniques, and the teacher feels the students are ready to take responsibility for leading the circles. Turning over the facilitation to her students, she divides the class in half and identifies student facilitators for each group, rotating facilitators on a regular basis.

After teaching terms and concepts such as impact, responsibility, and accountability, she feels students are ready to participate in accountability circles with a small group of students and anyone else who is impacted. The groups are usually numbered from three to six. Prompts such as: "I take responsibility for ____," and "When I ____, I impacted ____" are used. An example she shared was when several students swore. After exploring why people swear, students used the talking piece to respond to: "When I used the ____ word, I impacted ____." One student said he held himself accountable for laughing when someone else swore.

As these teachers contrast their use of classroom circle meetings and other restorative practices with more traditional and punitive discipline approaches they have used in the past, they believe that students feel more empowered to change their behaviors (and do change!) and are more reflective. They also comment that as teachers, they feel more positive and effective when using restorative practices rather than lecturing or scolding students for misbehaviors.

Scenario of Elementary/Middle School Collaboration Using Restorative Practices

When an incident involving three middle school students at an increasingly diverse, suburban elementary school surfaced, administrative staff and teachers at both schools decided to employ a collaborative, restorative approach. Their preplanning included a collaborative investigation, a meeting with staff from both schools, and a meeting with the students and their parents. It was important that everyone who would be part of the process agreed to the ground rules and norms for the upcoming restorative circle. While two of the families preferred the traditional, punitive approach, the third student's family supported the restorative approach and worked with school staff closely to ensure its effectiveness. The approach of the third family and staff is an example of a true partnership, with school staff willing to engage in critical conversations, a family interested in collaborating, and mutual respect for and from community members.[3] In addition, the learning process can be amplified to produce long-term positive changes.

The middle school students had trespassed onto the elementary school property on the weekend, taking safety cones and placing them in the formation of a swastika. The actions were caught on the school's security camera, and staff and students in the before-school care program discovered the symbol on the playground. The student's parents agreed to educate their son about the meaning of the swastika and the historical context. Prior to the restorative circle convening, the questions that would be posed were shared with the student and adults. When the restorative circle took place at the school, several staff from both schools and the district office, along with the student, his parents, and staff from the before-school care program, were present. Questions included:

- How were you impacted by the actions?
- What would need to happen for you to feel better?

Each time a question was asked, the talking piece was passed around the circle, with the talking limited to the person holding it. The student responded last by reflecting on what he had heard and adding any other information from his perspective. The result of the implementation of these practices was very successful. The student joined a student leadership group at the middle school, set up opportunities to volunteer at the elementary school and be a part of the community he impacted, and articulated his understanding of the impact of his actions and how his future behaviors would change. The student's family kept the talking piece as a reminder of the impact of his actions, his growth and learning during the discussion, and future goals.

Pause & Reflect: Are restorative practices something you'd like to learn more about? Can you see yourself implementing restorative practices in your school or classroom? How might you foster true partnerships between school and families where a collaborative approach is used in discipline situations?

After a Triggering Event

Matthew Kay, in his book *Not Light, but Fire*, describes a pop-up conversation strategy that you might consider after a significant disruption or event in your classroom, school, or community.[4] Examples might be a violent incident in the community or a racial incident that students witnessed at school. Kay recommends a judicious use of this strategy since it replaces the regular curriculum and, since it happens on the spur of the moment, the teacher has no time to prepare and plan for the conversation. But if the triggering event is urgent, it's impossible to ignore, or the benefit outweighs the risk, then this strategy may be helpful.

Kay suggests that first the students are asked to put all materials away, so that they can truly listen to one another without distractions. The teacher clarifies why the topic is important to spend a little time on, and that the class will return to the regular curriculum afterward. Next, students are invited to share one word to express how they are feeling or how they are doing as a result of the triggering event. Their responses might be captured in writing for the class to see, and time should be given to students to ask questions and elaborate. The teacher might comment on the feelings that were shared, asking the class to go out of their way to be kind to one another and lift each other up for the remainder of the day. Students could be given time to capture some of their thoughts in writing or drawings, and invited to share those with the teacher if they choose.

Pause & Reflect: When and how might this strategy be useful in your work with students or adults?

WHEN THINGS DON'T GO AS PLANNED WITH COLLEAGUES

This work is challenging for so many reasons, including divided political perspectives, values, and lived experiences. Inevitably, you will find yourself in situations where your words or actions are questioned by colleagues, or you experience resistance to the social justice work you are doing. In these situations, our initial words of advice are to lean in, ask questions, and be curious. Sometimes, but not always, being curious will open lines of communication and you and the other person(s) will all learn new information that could improve your relationships with each other.

You've probably found yourself in a situation at work when a colleague said something that offended you or others. It might have been a false statement or a comment that was racist, sexist, ableist, or hurtful. In the interest of preserving the relationships, many people tend to ignore these comments or pretend it didn't happen. However, our silence contributes to the inequities and lack of understanding that continue in our society. If we address hurtful comments in our classroom, let's address them outside of the classroom as well!

You will make a decision about whether to engage in the conversation after an offensive or uninformed remark, and it will depend on where it happened, when it happened, who was present, and how impactful it was. Waiting to address it at a later time is an option, and you may even want to schedule a private time to talk with the other person. There are also times when you may decide the conversation isn't worth your time and investment due to previous interactions. Remember that it's up to you to decide when to engage. There are some people in your midst who may have a closed mind, and anything you say will be dismissed. Dr. Caprice Hollins, one of our mentors, advises that our time is better spent conversing with those who are open to learning and being influenced.[5]

When an offensive or hurtful remark is made by a colleague that you decide to address, show interest in their thoughts and attitudes. A strategy we recommend is paraphrasing, pausing, and questioning (PPQ). When used together, in that order, PPQ shows the other person you are listening, hearing them, and curious to learn more. The following chapter provides explanation and examples of how this strategy is used. It is important that the questions you pose are genuine and demonstrate your curiosity. The intent is to try to understand where your colleague is coming from and to learn more about their perspective. Before you jump in with your own thoughts, giving your colleague time to process may help to temper the emotions and defuse the situation to some extent. Once you've given your colleague a chance to elaborate, you may find it appropriate to share some of your own perspective and knowledge. It could be that since you actively listened and showed your colleague you truly heard them, they will be able to hear you as well.

You may have heard the phrase: "Expect and accept nonclosure." This is pertinent here because it takes time for people's thinking to evolve. The goal isn't to change your colleague's mind immediately, but you're planting seeds, and if the conversation prompts them to be more reflective, then it's a big success!

Perhaps you've been the one who has offended someone else. This happens to most, maybe all of us at some point. It doesn't mean you are a bad person, but it does need to be acknowledged and dealt with. This situation is addressed in detail in the next chapter.

WHEN THINGS DON'T GO AS PLANNED WITH PARENTS/COMMUNITY MEMBERS

Parent/Caregiver Concerns

If you're familiar with Lucy Calkins's *Units of Study in Writing*, there is an entire book on "If . . . Then . . ." The purpose of Calkins's curriculum in this specific book is to offer suggestions to practitioners when supporting students in reading and writing.[6] In writing this book, we couldn't provide the same sort of "If . . . Then . . ." scenarios because the scenarios you will most likely encounter will be nonstop and exhausting. That said, our hope is to encourage you to engage in the following steps:

- Take a deep breath. This is real, hard, purposeful work you are doing. To do so, it is pertinent to center yourself.
- Revisit your *why*. This is your anchor.
- When questioned by families or community, as hard as it may be, don't take it personally. This is not about you. It is about the student-centered decisions you are enforcing. For some, this may bring discomfort, fear, and so forth. These are potentially new shifts that awaken uneasiness within someone. Celebrate that for what it is—movement.
- Lean in: the power of asking questions is vital in the moment. Ask clarifying questions. As you lean in, listen for glimpses of alignment in vision and thinking. Leap on that moment and leverage it in support of the direction you are hoping for.
- Listen for entry points about belonging. Most people will agree that students should feel a sense of belonging. Try to keep students at the center of the conversation. Don't we all want what is best for all students?

Example Topics

All Lives Matter

In an effort to show solidarity to the social unrest occurring in the world, a fellow teacher posts on social media: "Black Lives Matter" and in response a parent replies with: "Why do you say that? All Lives Matter!" How does one respond to this? In some way you may have found yourself wrestling with the same or a similar dilemma. How do you speak against racism as an educator? In short, here's how the educator responded: "Yes, all lives do matter. But in this context, we are referring to Black Lives Matter because Black people have been the victims of systematic and intentional oppression that has occurred and continues, thus the focus is on the Black Lives specifically."

"I don't want my child to feel guilty for being White."

The intent is not to teach children to feel guilty because their direct White ancestors may have supported enslaving Black people. The reality is that the history we've been taught hasn't been the full truth. The intent is for educators to teach authentic, complete, accurate history, and impress on students the need to reflect on the past and learn from previous mistakes, in order to make the future a world in which all people are equal, valued, and respected. The goal is not to have students feel guilty but to take responsibility for the future. Our hope is that students will feel empowered to make a difference!

"Teachers shouldn't display an LGBTQ rainbow flag in the classroom."

Know your state regulations and policies. These are great resources that you should anchor and refer to. Know your district equity policies. Do you feel confident that your district will support you in displaying the rainbow flag? If not, who might you contact to discuss this with? Know your student population. Knowing your student population means if you're in a more liberal environment, you will be in a different place than in a more conservative community. Above all, seek to understand how gender identity impacts the student experience at school.[7]

In conclusion, and regardless of the topic in question, you're playing chess and you want your moves to be strategic. Are you going for the king in one move, or are you utilizing your pawns, thinking strategically for the plays you might make? That might mean leaning in and actively listening at first, then engaging in more inquiry after some time has passed. Suggestions and action steps might be more successful once you've participated in conversations with others and collected tangible data such as student surveys or interviews. Take it day by day, moment by moment, conversation by conversation.

SUMMARY OF KEY POINTS FROM THIS CHAPTER

- Lean in, inquire, and be curious.
- Keep lines of communication open.
- Listen for entry points for teaching about equity and belonging.
- We are all learners who can repair harm we've caused and rebuild relationships.
- Expect and accept nonclosure.
- Your *why* is your purpose or the beliefs that inspire you to devote your time, energy, and passion to this work. Always keep your *why* in mind and be ready to share it with others.

NOTES

1. Hammond, Z. (2015). *Culturally responsive teaching and the brain: Promoting authentic engagement and rigor among culturally and linguistically diverse students,* p. 54. Thousand Oaks, CA: Corwin.

2. National Center for Restorative Justice (2023). Seattle, WA. Retrieved from https://www.nationalcenterforrestorativejustice.com

3. Kleinrock, L. (2021). *Start here, start now: A guide to antibias and antiracist work in your school community.* Portsmouth, NH: Heinemann.

4. Kay, M. (2018). *Not light, but fire: How to lead meaningful race conversations in the classroom.* Portsmouth, NH: Stenhouse.

5. Hollins, C. (2023). *Inside out: The equity leader's guide to undoing institutional racism.* Gabriola Island, BC: New Society.

6. Calkins, L. (2017). *A guide to the writing workshop: Intermediate grades.* Portsmouth, NH: Heinemann.

7. American Psychological Association Mental Health Primers (2023). *Students exploring gender identity.* Retrieved from https://www.apa.org/ed/schools/primer/gender-identity

6

Leading This Work

If not us, then who? If not now, then when?—John Lewis, Freedom Riders bus journey, 1961[1]

Our hope is that, after reading this text, you are emboldened to be a leader in this work, whether that is with your own students, professional colleagues, or within a school or district. Remember that changes are the result of many small steps. Small steps, when combined, add up to bigger steps . . . and big steps can lead to significant impact on the experiences of students.

You don't need to wait for a formal invitation to lead equity work in your building or with your colleagues—all of us must own this critical work. Rather than waiting to have courageous conversations until we feel completely comfortable, we need to lean in and learn along with our students and colleagues. Learning how students can shape not only their own learning but their broader communities is what will propel us toward a more just world.

In his book *Why We Can't Wait*, Dr. Martin Luther King Jr. describes the year of 1963 as the beginning of "the Negro revolution."[2] In it, he describes the historical events that led to the revolution—disappointment by the slow pace of school desegregation and civil rights legislation, to name a few. For Blacks during that time, hearing "wait" almost always meant "never." It was these reasons along with many others that created a sense of urgency within Blacks to unite in forming a nonviolent movement against racial segregation.

Schools today are facing and wrestling with their own "why we can't wait" moments. Teachers are supporting academic growth while addressing chronic absenteeism. They are exploring authentic opportunities to engage with families while creating culturally responsive classrooms that provide their community of learners with equitable, supportive, and welcoming learning environments. These important factors create a sense of urgency for exploring and implementing wraparound approaches to supporting students more holistically and authentically.

It is up to all of us to share responsibility for this work, not just when we discuss equity, but in using an equity lens to frame all that we do. Being vulnerable and modeling lifelong learning empowers others to do the same. We align with Ruth Bader Ginsburg in her 2015 Harvard address that we should "fight for the things that you care about, but do it in a way that will lead others to join you."[3] Our goal is to call people into the work of promoting social justice. The equity momentum is moving forward. The ball is moving, and do you find yourself ahead of the ball, beside the ball, or behind the ball?

We believe this work is both deeply professional and deeply personal, and it begins with ourselves. We work against the notion that leadership requires titles or certifications—anyone can be a leader. Leadership requires personal reflection, vulnerability, a clear vision, passion, and a commitment to improvement. Leadership requires courage.

In the appendix section, we have included a personal reflection tool to help you identify areas of celebration and growth; see appendix C: "Leading with an Equity Lens."

START WITH SELF

Continue Your Own Personal Journey

There are many ways to continue doing the internal work of diversity and equity. We recommend that you remain mindful and honest about the biases and stereotypes you hold as you keep reading, watching documentaries, listening to podcasts, and attending classes and events that offer opportunities to hear from different perspectives. Converse with others about issues of race and equity; seek to understand their perspectives. Learning more about the roots of inequality and oppression in this country, for example, can be eye opening for many who haven't experienced issues such as systemic racism or generational poverty.

Set yearly (or half-yearly) goals for deepening your understanding. What concepts do you want to learn more about? What resources are you interested in learning? Have an accountability partner, someone you check in with on a regular basis to share your progress toward your goals. Share what you are learning with friends and colleagues. Challenge one another's thinking; celebrate successes.

> Pause & Reflect: What books, documentaries, or other resources have influenced your thinking about diversity, equity, and inclusion? How have they shaped your thinking? What shifts are you making in your practice as a result of your new learning?

Examine Your Privilege

Be open and honest with yourself about your privilege and the ways in which your own identity has shaped who you are as an educator. You might find it helpful to engage in an identity map activity, where you look at the different identity markers that you have—both invisible and visible—and reflect on how you have personally experienced varying layers of privilege and oppression.[4] As of 2019, White women make up the vast majority (80 percent) of the teaching workforce.[5] Even as our school communities continue to diversify, the demographic of teachers continues to be racially, culturally, and linguistically homogeneous, for the most part.[6] This phenomenon is not due to chance. Until the opening of labor markets to women and minorities, teaching was one of the few occupations that women might select alongside social work, nursing, and clerical work.[7] Diversifying the teaching workforce continues to be a focus of policymakers, teacher preparation programs, and researchers. However, barriers to entry (certifications, degrees, and testing) coupled with a modest salary often means that entrance into teaching signifies some level of privilege or access. We need to acknowledge and unpack the impact of the discrepancy between the workforce and the students we serve.

Return to the first chapter of this text to revisit what identity means as you continue to reflect on your own work. Start now by leaning into the work—don't wait until you have all the answers, because you never will. And always stay the course. Our world needs you as part of this important work.

Uncover Your Own Biases and Stereotypes

We all have implicit biases and stereotypes; identifying them enables us to mitigate them. Biases and stereotypes affect our own behaviors and have an impact on others, even if our intentions are not overt. Stereotype threat is a psychological threat in which people are or feel themselves to be at risk of conforming to stereotypes about their social group. Stereotypes can undermine the performance of people who are the target of the stereotype. Zaretta Hammond describes stereotype threat this way: "It happens when a student becomes anxious about his inadequacy as a learner because he believes his failure on an assignment or test will confirm the negative stereotype associated with his race, socioeconomic status, gender, or language background (i.e., Black kids aren't good at math; Spanish speakers can't develop academic language)."[8]

An example of this is documented in *Whistling Vivaldi* by Claude Steele, who shares the results of a study at the University of Michigan on the impact of negative stereotypes of women's ability in math.[9] Men and women were recruited for the study who had strong goals and expectations for themselves in math and had always been good in math. During the study, half of the females were told the test detected gender differences, and the other half were told the test did *not* detect gender differences. The females who were told it couldn't detect gender differences performed well in comparison to their male counterparts. However, the women who were told the test did show gender differences, which reminded them of the threat of stereotypes, underperformed in relation to the men.

Stereotype threat is theorized to be a factor in both racial and gender gaps in academic achievement. In the words of Claude Steele: "[Stereotype threat] can contribute to some of our most vexing personal and societal problems, but . . . doing quite feasible things to reduce this threat can lead to dramatic improvements in these problems."[10]

If you haven't taken the Implicit Association Test from Loyola Marymount University, which measures the strength of associations between concepts, revealing one's subconscious or implicit attitudes toward groups of people, we encourage you to do so as a way of uncovering your biases and stereotypes.[11]

Pause & Reflect: What biases show up for you in your practice? How do they influence the way you show up? Based on that, what shifts are necessary?

Be a Role Model; Lean In

Teachers and staff in schools are influencers and mentors. Whether students admit it or not, they take cues from the adults in their midst. How those adults respond to instances of injustice can support positive changes or perpetuate systemic bias and systems of privilege.

It is not uncommon for White teachers and staff to look the other way when they hear racist remarks or witness offensive behaviors. They may feel unprepared to intervene, worried about doing the wrong thing or making the situation worse. However, silence communicates acceptance, and if the adults don't respond to injustices, students may feel that the unjust behavior is acceptable, thus being retraumatized. POC have shared that when instances of racism are ignored over and over, they liken it to *death by a thousand cuts*.

Microaggressions, as defined by Zaretta Hammond, are "the subtle, everyday verbal and nonverbal slights, snubs, or insults which communicate hostile, derogatory, or negative messages to people of color based solely on their marginalized group membership."[12] A single microaggression or instance of racism by itself can be overwhelming, but the cumulative effect of many minor events adds up to trauma.

On May 25, 2020, George Floyd, a forty-six-year-old Black man, was murdered in Minneapolis, Minnesota, by Derek Chauvin, a forty-four-year-old White police officer. At some point in their lives, both were students in an elementary school setting. We don't know what their educational experiences were, but perhaps if their experiences had included more opportunities to engage in conversations around issues of race, the outcome could have been different. School may be the only place where students can be supported in understanding and celebrating differences.

If teachers and other educators avoid challenging conversations about race, identity, or empathy, the message may be that those topics aren't important or valued. This also applies to interactions with other adults. If we bypass conversations about race, it perpetuates the White dominance that exists in our society, and we can't address racism if we don't acknowledge it. Additionally, teaching students about race and racism equips them to better understand the world they live in.

Teaching students directly and openly about race and racism promotes understanding and self-awareness. It is an important step toward a more equitable and just future. Pamela taught a kindergarten class about race, using the book *Our Skin: A First Conversation about Race*, and it is an example of direct teaching that can make a big difference in how students approach race.[13] She began the lesson by explaining that the lesson was about a serious topic—race and racism. The students were asked to reflect on the color of their own skin, and were introduced to terms such as melanin, POC, and racism. As Pamela read about how racism can be a rule, she asked students to think about rules that could be unfair. Examples shared included: "Only friends who sit at the red table can go to recess," "Only the friends who are in the back can go to the library," and "Only girls with blond hair can be princesses." Students wrote or sketched their examples on sticky notes to be compiled on a class visual. At the conclusion of the lesson, students were reminded that an untrue or unfair rule (or even a "made-up rule") should be talked about. Pamela shared an example of anti-racism: "I see you at recess playing with all kinds of other friends that have different colors of skin. That's anti-racism because it is treating others fairly and respectfully." The book concludes with a message that by changing unfair rules, by teaching, helping, learning, and listening, we can all work toward racial justice and treating people fairly.

Demonstrate through your words and actions that your classroom and school is a place where all students, staff, and visitors are respected and included, a place where everyone belongs. Avoid silence and lean in to these critical conversations because what we do today has an impact on what our students do in the future.

Pause & Reflect: In what ways will you model the behaviors and attitudes that you'd like your students and colleagues to exemplify? How will you lean into situations where you've witnessed an injustice? How will you directly teach students about race and racism?

VISION AND LEARNING-CENTERED APPROACHES

Leaders focused on diversity, equity, and inclusion (DEI) must shape a vision and employ approaches that underscore a commitment to the success of every child and adult.

Articulate a Clear Vision

Know why you are engaging in this work. Clearly and continuously communicate it, as well as your strategic plan for meeting your goals and vision, to stakeholders (both internal and external). Engage other diverse stakeholders in the creation of your vision. Monitor your vision frequently—are your activities in line with your vision for moving equity forward in your classroom, building, district, or program?

Boldly Assert the Importance of Key Beliefs

For many learners, it is hard to overcome low expectations. Due to inherent biases, some educators may have low expectations for student performance and may subconsciously accept mediocre performance as the norm. Teaching is not a hobby, and we cannot perpetuate low expectations. It can't be something we do just for fun. If you're in education, it's because you have a conviction and belief that you can positively impact student achievement *and* influence the paths of students. All educators, from paraprofessionals to superintendents to researchers, must be committed to doing whatever it takes in service of every student and the needs that surface. In order to empower educators to improve learning experiences for these students, leaders need to give voice to three underlying beliefs:

- *All* students can learn.
- Students need opportunities to own their learning *so they believe they can learn.*
- All students can learn at high standards.

As Zaretta Hammond explains in *Culturally Responsive Teaching and the Brain*, our ultimate goal as culturally responsive educators is to help dependent learners become independent learners, thus owning their own learning.[14] In order for that to happen, students need agency, or the belief that they *can* learn. Leaders need to be relentless in establishing nonnegotiable, academically rigorous standards for each student, modeling these tenets themselves, communicating them often, and reinforcing and communicating them at every opportunity.

Approach the Work So That Others Will Want to Join You

You're no doubt familiar with public shaming on social media or in real life, and if you've ever been the target of such shaming, it feels pretty awful, doesn't it? If your goal is to expand DEI work, avoiding a shame-and-blame approach can be a much more invitational approach for others to join you. In our experience in leading equity work, it has been more effective to promote an open learning environment rather than one that alienates. Loretta J. Ross, professor at Smith College, has an enlightening TED talk for productive conversations titled "Don't Call Them Out, Call Them In" where she shares strategies that create space for growth.[15] She promotes productive conversations as opposed to conversations that push people out. She contrasts the difference between a response such as: "I can't believe you just said that. You're sexist [or racist, toxic, manipulative]," and a response such as: "I beg your pardon. I know you are a caring person. How can I reconcile what you just said with the kind person I know you to be?"

As a White woman, Emilie experienced a range of initial responses to the DEI focus that was introduced in two school districts, reactions varying from embracing the work to denying that there were any problems. The topic of White privilege was particularly challenging for some White colleagues to acknowledge. Some were hesitant to engage for fear of being shamed and blamed. Since the district's goals were to promote awareness, knowledge, and skills in becoming more culturally competent, an invitational approach was used, one in which even the experts and consultants acknowledged room for growth. Inviting questions, raising concerns and sharing fears were all part of the "we are all learners" approach. Listening to one another and being genuinely curious were strategies that proved highly beneficial in demonstrating that our purposes were to learn, not to blame.

A Black colleague wisely said: "We should care less about assigning blame, and more about teaching responsibility for the future." With an invitational approach, you are likely to bring people along with you in your journey.

Pause & Reflect: Consider the ways in which you engage others, especially when you hold different perspectives. Do you tend to "call out" or "call in"?

Pace and Lead

Be deliberate about the pace of this work. You want a pace that communicates a sense of urgency, while being sustainable at the same time. Maintaining a spotlight on equity throughout the year is important, and with limited time, make a plan for how you can create a consistent focus.

Some organizations plan DEI training to take place two or three times a year. Understanding that time for professional development is limited, how can leaders bridge the gaps between those training sessions? To build continuity and sustain the learning, consider weaving the focus into other topics at staff meetings. Topics such as social-emotional learning, inclusion, mental health, and instructional practice all lend themselves to integration with equity.

Embedding messages, quotes, or resource recommendations in newsletters, emails, or other forms of communication can demonstrate an ongoing commitment to equity. Highlighting positive examples from staff or students goes a long way toward underscoring your goals without taking time away from other competing commitments.

Pause & Reflect: How will you bridge the gaps between professional development sessions in order to maintain focus on equity efforts at your school or organization?

Communicate DEI as a Journey

Keep in mind that diversity, equity, and inclusion work is challenging and it requires a significant investment of time and energy. It is a journey, not an event or destination. It is a marathon, not a sprint. Help others to see that this is not one-and-done type of initiative. DEI work is an imperative response to addressing historical marginalizations and a step toward meeting the needs of the students in front of us today. It must be woven into the fabric of our institutions. DEI work needs to be living work, constantly revisited, revised, and improved. For this reason, DEI work must show up in every facet of education, instruction practice, curriculum, hiring and recruitment practices, professional development, family engagement, classroom management, and discipline. Equity is a lens that needs to be applied at all times, in all places.

Pause & Reflect: What ideas in this section (Vision and Learning-Centered Approaches) resonate with you?

WORKING WITH OTHERS

For this work to move forward, we must also become comfortable opening up about race, gender, ethnicity, and other identity markers both with colleagues as well as students. It is especially critical for educators who are White to continue to engage in reflective, internal work about how race and gender impact practice. It can't be that we constantly rely on our POC colleagues to start conversations about identity and privilege.

Listen, Engage, and Amplify the Voices of People of Color

Active listening to people who are different, especially people who have experienced systems of oppression, is essential, but even more so for folks who have experienced varying degrees of privilege. Practice viewing your colleagues, students, and community through an asset lens, where all backgrounds, experiences, and knowledge are seen as valuable.

Listen to concerns, follow through, and keep the conversation moving. Perhaps one of the biggest mistakes we make as leaders is listening to respond, rather than truly listening. Particularly in matters that are highly personal, it can be natural to defend one's decision-making, but we urge leaders to make every attempt to truly hear those who may have differences of opinion and different experiences. Leaning in and being curious can keep you engaged in the work and support growth forward.

Ensure that the voices of POC (students, staff, and families) are amplified. Are POC represented on committees and in decision-making processes? Are their experiences validated? Are students of color empowered to engage in discussions with each other? Are students of color provided with opportunities to authentically lead in their schools and communities?

Pause & Reflect: Think about the people and groups you interact with. How many of those people and groups have different identities from you? How can you widen your sphere of influence to learn from others who hold different perspectives? How can voices of POC be amplified in your work?

Have Courageous Conversations

Having courageous conversations in the "public square"—a statement often used by Emily Amick on Instagram (@emilyinyourphone)—is another way to move this work forward and broaden the perspectives of those we come into contact with.[16] Public square conversations might be informal conversations, posts, and comments on social media or public forums, or speaking out at events. Communicating where you stand on social issues can be a first step in connecting with others or nudging someone's thinking.

In addition to the formal opportunities to learn about equity and diversity, intentional reflection on your own identity and experiences is key. Start by looking at your own identity and layers of privilege. As professor James Gee has said, we all walk around with an "identity kit" that is tied to the language that we use.[17] For example, consider your speech, housing, clothing, type of transportation, access to education, if and where you vacation, and how and where you get groceries—does this give you any insight into privileges that you may hold?

Be Mindful of *Intent versus Impact*

We will all offend others from time to time. No matter how reflective we are, how open to learning and committed to social justice we are, we will offend other people, usually unintentionally. When this happens, be mindful of intent versus impact. The impact we have on others is more important than our intent.

When you have offended someone, focus on your impact by asking the person to explain. Use openers such as: "Please help me understand how you are feeling," "How did what I said offend you?," and "I want to understand my impact; can you say more about what you mean?" By opening up genuine conversation, you are showing that you value the other person's feelings and thoughts, and it gives the person a chance to process the impact of your action. As much as possible, try not to be defensive. Instead, listen and learn, and thank them for taking the risk to engage with you.

Be Vulnerable

When leading this work, model that you don't have all the answers. Be open to vulnerability and model continual reflection—it is okay, and even powerful, to be uncomfortable when having critical conversations. When things come up in your setting that you are unsure how to address, share them with trusted colleagues. Your own vulnerability will help build empathy within your team, and this empathy is necessary to build trust.

Brené Brown says that "empathy is connecting to the emotions that underpin an experience."[18] When discussing identity and experience, a group of people—especially when it is a diverse group of people—will have various lived experiences. While the group will not necessarily share those experiences, a mutual empathy is needed to move the group forward. Vulnerability, empathy, and trust are thus cyclical.

Admit mistakes, as these will inevitably happen. Holding ourselves to a high standard, and having the vulnerability to admit when we have been wrong, builds trust within leadership. We will all make mistakes as we continue to learn, and perhaps look back and wish that we had handled a situation differently. While we hold ourselves accountable, this work also demands that we hold each other accountable. If a colleague or staff member makes an ignorant or uninformed remark, inviting them into a conversation with dignity (i.e., "calling them in") is a strategy we recommend, being sure that the staff member isn't ostracized or shamed for their comment.

Examples of ways we might address an ignorant or hurtful comment from a colleague or community member include:

- Ask the staff member to tell you more about their line of thinking.
- Explain how the comment made you feel, while recognizing that may not have been the intent of the speaker.
- Take some time to process, and then have a private conversation with the staff member.
- Share a resource (film, article, podcast, etc.) that has helped shift your thinking on a similar issue.

If you are in a leadership role, you might also consider seeking feedback. If you choose to do so, be sincere about seeking feedback, and seek it often. Of course, as a staff member, receiving formal feedback is embedded in your duties. Beyond educator evaluations, you might consider surveying colleagues and students about their experiences with you and their understanding of your commitment to equity. Educator Liz Kleinrock periodically surveys students about their experiences in her classroom, and creates visual graphs of responses to unpack as a classroom community.[19] For students, posing questions about whether they feel safe, heard, and respected in school spaces is key.

Prior to soliciting any feedback from others, you'll want to consider whether you really want the feedback, and what you hope to learn from it. Demonstrating what you hope to gain from this feedback will determine the sincerity with which it is given.

Paraphrase, Pause, Question: Do You Believe in Magic?

Arthur Costa and Robert Garmston, authors of *Cognitive Coaching: Foundations for Renaissance Schools*, and Connie Hoffman, all three experts in leadership strategies, had profound influences on Emilie's education and leadership skills.[20] One of the communication strategies that she often refers to as "magic" is paraphrasing, pausing, and questioning, or PPQ for short. Sometimes misunderstanding arises because there's a disconnect between what we think a person said and what they were actually trying to get across. We may jump to a conclusion without first checking to see if we're on the right track. Using the strategy of PPQ can help to avoid that trap because it communicates: "I'm trying to understand you, and your perspective is important."

We have found that simply by paraphrasing, a person's emotion or anger was often reduced; they understood they were being heard and could start to engage in conversation. We have found this to be true in working with students, colleagues, parents, and family. Pausing briefly and following up with a question helps you check for understanding, build or strengthen a relationship, and show that your intent is to truly appreciate the other person's perspective.

What is PPQ? A paraphrase is a statement that communicates what you heard or understood, and is best structured in the form of a "you" statement. The pronoun "I" can elevate your own thoughts and indicate that you're going to insert your own ideas. Using a paraphrase builds trust and signals that you care enough to want to understand what the other person is communicating. Examples of paraphrase stems include:

- You're wondering about the effect of . . .
- You're concerned about your students' behaviors when . . .
- So you're thinking that once you've introduced lessons on Black history . . .
- You're worried that your students' parents might . . .
- So you are questioning the intent of . . .

The second P in PPQ is pause, or silence. We've learned that when students or adults are provided with a wait time of three seconds or *less*, their responses are shorter and less developed. Giving people three seconds or *more* allows crucial time to think . . . which tends to open up dialogue and support more in-depth thought processes. People need the chance to do their own thinking, and if given that pause, many people will see that you trust them to formulate their own ideas and responses.

The last third of the PPQ strategy is questioning. Questions that use tentative language tend to put the other person more at ease, and seem more invitational. Using plural forms in questions communicates that there are multiple approaches or ideas, rather than one correct response. Some examples of questions using tentative language and/or plural forms are:

- *If you* used that strategy, how would you anticipate others to respond?
- How *might* you address this?
- If you could revisit this conversation, what *strategies* would you consider?
- What were *some of* the experiences you've had that caused you to feel this way?
- *Can you share* a little more about how you're feeling?
- I'm not sure I'm clear about what you're saying. *Could you* help me understand?

Questions without being preceded by a paraphrase and pause may be perceived as interrogation, and may shut down or limit the dialogue. Questions can take the form of probing for details, asking for elaboration, or seeking clarification.

Action Item: In your next uncomfortable conversation, try implementing the PPQ strategy. Start small with the first P (paraphrase) and continue to add on.

Consider Formal and Informal Roles

Formal roles might include an equity or DEI committee, or a lead role in your building. Informal roles are also important and might include professional book clubs, informal research, or even casual conversations with colleagues. We view anyone who is doing their own personal work, having courageous conversations, and advocating change at a small- or large-scale level as a leader in equity.

Establish a Core Team

The effectiveness of your equity efforts will be stronger if shared, and the end result will be better if many minds have influenced the direction. This may take the form of an equity team, or if your school has a leadership team that is already established, it may make sense to embed DEI work into that group's mission.

Membership in an equity team could include certificated staff, classified staff, parents, students, and community members. The group's purpose could be to set the vision, goals, and action plans for the school. As the group unpacks and analyzes issues of equity and belonging through an equity needs assessment, they can collaborate to develop plans for how changes are implemented. An example is the group could serve as a "think tank" in helping to develop responses to concerns and questions that arise from parents, students, and staff.

Suggestions for supporting the group's effectiveness include encouraging questioning among the group members, validating members, keeping notes, and holding regular meetings throughout the year. Some equity teams choose to have a book club as part of their collaboration, and other staff members may want to join in. Make sure to create an action plan for how the new learning will impact student experiences.

Your core team can be a significant part of keeping yourself energized. This type of work is challenging and, at times, discouraging. Equity work is also exciting and is one of the most important priorities that educators can have. Having others around you to validate your efforts, raise new ideas, question the action steps, and listen when you need a sounding board can be critical to continued success.

An important reminder is to share the work of the core team with the larger staff so that everyone is informed and invited to contribute.

Consider Leading a Diverse Book Club for Students

McKay, a fifth-grade teacher, has implemented a highly popular, voluntary Diverse Book Club for students that meets once a month during lunchtime. Students come from multiple fifth-grade classrooms, bringing their lunches, and McKay provides hot chocolate or other treats. In the informal, comfortable classroom atmosphere, he reads a carefully preselected story about diverse people, and lively discussion ensues during and after the read-aloud. Students feel at ease to share ideas, concerns, or questions with the group, and this type of choice activity supports those students in learning more about their own and other people's identities. Students leave the sessions energized, probably due to being heard, validated, and challenged to work toward social justice. An appreciation for differences is a thread that McKay is sure to weave through each session.

During one of the sessions, the read-aloud is Joanna Ho's book *Eyes That Kiss in the Corners*, a story about an Asian girl and her family.[21] One Chinese American student explains a wealth of background information and connections to the story, highlighting how students enrich the learning for everyone by bringing their own cultural experiences into the discussions. Toward the end of this particular book club session, a student's comment is poignant: "Not everyone is the same. I think we should embrace our differences, embrace who we are." Such wisdom coming from an eleven-year-old!

McKay gives up his lunch period once a month to provide this Diverse Book Club experience for students in his grade level. While we are not suggesting that this is the only way to provide this type of experience, it is an incredibly supportive structure for students, one that could perhaps be shared by multiple staff members or administrators.

Understand That Everyone Participates and Processes Differently

Just as we would provide multiple ways for students to engage with a topic and in a conversation, we should allow our colleagues to do the same (through whole group, small group, journaling, private conversation, etc.). As you plan your lessons or meetings, consider times during the meeting where there can be *options* for engagement. Or better yet, ask the person how they would like to engage.

Empower Others and Build a Succession Plan

As much as possible, bring in others as you plan and create professional development for staff. Support others to build their own leadership skills by inviting them to be co-presenters in presentations. Just like we try to use a gradual release of responsibility with students, bringing colleagues into equity leadership by inviting them to team with you is one way to help them take those first steps.

Delegate responsibilities such as committee leadership and activity planning. At one elementary school we visited, staff members were asked to help conduct interviews with students of color in order to set equity goals for the school. This gave those staff members a personal and up-close experience in listening to authentic student voices, which in turn influenced their own sense of urgency about the development of goals.

Pause & Reflect: If you were to leave your organization, who would step up to lead the work?

Prioritize Self-Care

One of our mentors, Dr. Caprice Hollins, says: "Leading equity work is emotionally, physically, and mentally exhausting to the point where there will be days you will feel as though you have been struck by a moving vehicle."[22] She advocates, as we do, that self-care is essential in order to sustain your focus and commitment.

What does it mean to prioritize self-care? In order for this work to be sustainable, you need to invest in self-preservation! Some of the strategies we've found most helpful are:

- Find one or more thinking partners who are also doing equity work, people you can call on when you need support.
- Continue learning, reading, attending conferences, watching documentaries. These things can help fuel your passion and keep you focused on *why* this work you are doing is important.

- Set boundaries on how many days/hours you will devote to this work, so that you can reserve some time with family, time for hobbies and relaxation.
- Accept help that is offered, and delegate responsibility to others. Remember that you don't have to do everything yourself, and delegating supports others in developing their own leadership skills.
- Keep the values of appreciation and gratitude in mind. Lifting *others* up has the effect of lifting *yourself* up. Being grateful for what you have has a positive effect on your overall well-being in addition to specific medical conditions such as brain injury, stroke, and brain tumors.[23]

ADVOCATE FOR A FORMAL EQUITY POLICY FOR YOUR SCHOOL DISTRICT OR ORGANIZATION

It has been our experience that many educators feel nervous about entering into conversations about race and equity. Possible reasons for this nervousness are insecurity about their ability to answer questions from students, anticipated concerns from parents or community members, or not having prior experience in having these types of courageous conversations. One way to support teachers and other educators in engaging in this work is to support the development of an equity policy and/or an equity lens for your organization.

Tony Davis, director of equity and family partnerships in the Tahoma School District, underscores the importance of a strong policy or lens: "The components that I feel are most important to moving equity forward are a Superintendent and School Board who support the work, and an Equity Policy or Lens used across the organization that specifies that all students need to feel welcome, safe, supported, and included." Teachers and staff who are working in systems with these components in place know that the system has their backs. Employees can point to the equity policy or lens as third points when facing criticism or concerns from parents, students, or community members. Davis adds: "At the end of the day, what's important is keeping all students safe, welcome, supported and included. And 'every' means 'every.'"

Pause & Reflect: Does your school or organization have an equity policy or lens? If not, how might you collaborate with others to move in that direction?

Celebrate Success

Sometimes we are so busy getting things accomplished that we neglect to find time to celebrate our successes. Even the small steps toward goals are worthy of celebrating. Make reminders on your calendar periodically with a notation: "What can we celebrate?" You may want to start meetings by mentioning a few celebrations, or you might share celebrations in written communications.

Even a short positive comment on a sticky note to an individual (e.g., "Great job of including a land acknowledgment in your training," "Congrats on being courageous in sharing your truth in our meeting today," or "Your response to a concerned parent really showed sincere curiosity") can make a huge impact and give others energy to continue the work. Your colleagues and community will appreciate the acknowledgment, reflection, and thanks.

Pause & Reflect: What opportunities can you provide to celebrate success with your students or colleagues?

SUMMARY OF KEY POINTS FROM THIS CHAPTER

- It is up to all of us to share responsibility in promoting equity. Lean into the work.
- Continue learning about DEI, reflect on your own privilege, and uncover your biases.
- Use an invitational approach so that others will want to join you in this work.
- Apply an equity lens at all times.
- As you have courageous conversations, showing humility and vulnerability will help build empathy and trust.
- Employ effective communication skills: paraphrase, pause, question.
- Consider formal and informal roles for people supporting the DEI focus.
- Remember to take time for self-care.
- Advocate for (or support) an equity policy for your organization.
- Celebrate success!

CHAPTER 6 RESOURCES: LEADING THIS WORK

- "Discussion Prompts for Supporting Identity, Empathy, and Advocacy" (appendix B): Sample questions to ask your students during discussions to promote deep thinking about identity, perspective, and empathy, as well as questions that may prompt students to consider advocating for a more just world.
- "Leading with an Equity Lens: A Reflection Tool for Educational Leaders" (appendix C): A tool to assist with reflecting on your own practice from a critical lens. This can help leaders examine aspects of leading in order to identify areas of strength and areas for improvement, set goals, and monitor progress. Intentionally pondering these questions may help you and your organization to make better decisions for all stakeholders.
- *Our Skin: A First Conversation about Race* by Megan Madison, Jessica Ralli, and Isabel Roxas (2021)

NOTES

1. Suggs, E. (2019, December 29). Five things to know about Congressman John Lewis. *Atlanta Journal-Constitution.* Retrieved from https://www.ajc.com/news/five-things-know-about-congressman-john-lewis/uzHfUBLepoRaRnwvjlmpkK/
2. King Jr., M. L. (2000). *Why we can't wait.* London: Penguin.
3. Vagianos, A. (2015, June 2). *Ruth Bader Ginsburg tells young women: "Fight for the things you care about."* Harvard Radcliffe Institute. Retrieved from https://www.radcliffe.harvard.edu/news-and-ideas/ruth-bader-ginsburg-tells-young-women-fight-for-the-things-you-care-about
4. Kleinrock, L. (2021). *Start here, start now: A guide to antibias and antiracist work in your school community.* Portsmouth, NH: Heinemann.
5. Plachowski, T. J. (2019). Reflections of preservice teachers of color: Implications for the teacher demographic diversity gap. *Education Sciences, 9*(2), 144.
6. Little, J. W., & Bartlett, L. (2010). The teacher workforce and problems of educational equity. *Review of Research in Education, 34*(1), 285–328.
7. Yellen, J. L. (2020, May). *The history of women's work and wages and how it has created success for us all.* The Brookings Institution. Retrieved from https://www.brookings.edu/essay/the-history-of-womens-work-and-wages-and-how-it-has-created-success-for-us-all/#:~:text=Between%20the%201930s%20and%20mid,factors%20contributed%20to%20this%20rise
8. Hammond. Z. (2015). *Culturally responsive teaching and the brain: Promoting authentic engagement and rigor among culturally and linguistically diverse students,* p. 91. Thousand Oaks, CA: Corwin.
9. Steele, C. (2010). *Whistling Vivaldi: How stereotypes affect us and what we can do.* New York: Norton.

10. Steele, C. (2010). *Whistling Vivaldi: How stereotypes affect us and what we can do*, p. 11. New York: Norton.

11. Loyola Marymount University Implicit Bias Task Force. (2016). *Test your implicit bias—Implicit Association Test (IAT)*. Retrieved from https://www.resources .lmu.edu/dei/initiativesprograms/implicitbiasinitiative/whatisimplicitbias/

12. Hammond. Z. (2015). *Culturally responsive teaching and the brain: Promoting authentic engagement and rigor among culturally and linguistically diverse students*, p. 47. Thousand Oaks, CA: Corwin.

13. Madison, M., Ralli, J., & Roxas, I. (2021). *Our skin: A first conversation about race*. New York: Rise.

14. Hammond. Z. (2015). *Culturally responsive teaching and the brain: Promoting authentic engagement and rigor among culturally and linguistically diverse students*. Thousand Oaks, CA: Corwin.

15. Ross, L. (2021). *Don't call people out—call them in* [Video]. TED talk. Retrieved from https://www.youtube.com/watch?v=xw_720iQDss

16. Amick, E. [@emilyinyourphone]. (n.d.). Posts [Instagram profile]. Instagram. Retrieved April 30, 2023, from https://www.instagram.com/emilyinyourphone

17. Gee, J. P. (2005). *An introduction to discourse analysis*. New York: Routledge.

18. Brown, B. (2015). *Daring greatly: How the courage to be vulnerable transforms the way we live, love, parent, and lead*, p. 118. New York: Avery.

19. Kleinrock, L. (2021). *Start here, start now: A guide to antibias and antiracist work in your school community*. Portsmouth, NH: Heinemann.

20. Costa, A., & Garmston, R. (2002). *Cognitive coaching: A foundation for renaissance schools*. Norwood, MA: Christopher-Gordon.

21. Ho, J. (2021). *Eyes that kiss in the corners*. New York: HarperCollins.

22. Hollins, C. (2023). *Inside out: The equity leader's guide to undoing institutional racism*. Gabriola Island, BC: New Society.

23. Johns Hopkins University. (2023). *The power of positive thinking*. Retrieved from https://www.hopkinsmedicine.org/health/wellness-and-prevention/the -power-of-positive-thinking

Appendix A
Building a Robust, Diverse Classroom Library

Utilize your public library. Check out as many books as you're able to.

Utilize your school library, and partner with your school librarian to curate collections to rotate into your classroom. Your librarian may know of other resources to access.

List titles you'd like to add; then include them in a "Wish List for Our Classroom" with a newsletter or other parent communication. Doing this just prior to the holidays might give parents great ideas that can benefit the whole classroom. Including a diversity of titles and topics will garner more interest!

Apply for teacher grants through your PTSA or school district. You might even consider creating a Donors Choose request.

If you use book orders from one of the companies that sell to schools, use your points to acquire books on identity, empathy, and advocacy for your library.

Peruse used bookstores for appropriate titles.

Share your wish list with your school administration. Administrators sometimes have the opportunity to respond to these types of requests (for all classrooms), particularly toward the end of a budget cycle.

Some organizations (such as First Book) review applications to purchase sets of books for classrooms.

Library sales are great places to augment your classroom libraries. Many public libraries have one or more sales a year.

Collaborate with your colleagues, perhaps sharing collections on a rotating basis.

Appendix B
Discussion Prompts for Supporting Identity, Empathy, and Advocacy

Choose questions (or add your own) that fit the story you've chosen to read.

BEFORE READING THE TEXT

- As you look at the title, and the pictures on the front and back covers, what would you infer this story might be about? What clues did you use to make your inference?
- As I read this story, pay attention to how the characters show empathy [or kindness, curiosity, bravery, persistence, etc.].
- As you listen to this story, think about what the characters do to show respect for people who are different from them.
- As I read this story, put your thumb up if you notice _____ [courage, empathy, respect, kindness, etc.].

DURING THE READING

- The author included characters with different skin colors in this story. Why do you think they decided to do that?
- What do you notice about the skin colors in this story? Are there characters [representations] missing from the story? If so, who is missing?
- What do you think the author means by _____?

- Why is this illustration important to the story?
- Why do you think the author said _____?
- From the clues in the story, how would you imagine _____ [character] is feeling?
- What are you noticing?
- Who is taking action in this story? What are they doing?

AFTER THE READING

- Is this story like any others we've read? In what ways?
- What did you notice about the illustrations in this text/story? How did they contribute to the story?
- In what ways are you similar or different from the main character in this story?
- What habits of mind [traits] did the main character demonstrate? (Examples: courage, persistence, empathy, inquisitiveness, honesty, confusion, creativity, curiosity)
- Authors usually have a message they are communicating in their stories. What do you think the author's message is? What evidence in the story supports that message?
- How important do you think the author's message is? Why?
- In what ways do you think this message is important?
- Is there anything you will change as a result of thinking about this story?
- What impact did this story have on you?
- Was there anything in this story that surprised you? Explain your thinking.
- How can you relate this text/story to your own experiences?
- If the main character/protagonist were here in our classroom today, what might you want to ask them?
- Do you think this story is important for other children to hear? Why or why not?
- The character(s) in this story tried to make the world a better place. What could YOU do to make the world a better place?

Appendix C
Leading with an Equity Lens: A Reflection Tool for Educators

As you consider your teaching and leadership style, priorities, and actions, reflect on the extent to which you demonstrate these behaviors. Using a 5 (consistently) to a 1 (not yet), indicate how often you exhibit these examples of leading with an equity lens. Use this tool again later in the same year to monitor progress.

5—Consistently   4—Most of the time   3—Some of the time   2—Rarely
1—Not yet

Action/Behavior	DATE:_____	DATE:_____
	Frequency	Frequency
Students are greeted each day in ways that show respect for them as students.		
My classroom (or school) library is updated with rich literature that features characters and information from diverse cultures and backgrounds.		
Students' identities are valued in my classroom and school curricula and activities.		
Visuals in my classroom and around my school clearly show that we value diversity (diversity of people, cultural diversity).		

Action/Behavior	DATE:_____	DATE:_____
	Frequency	Frequency
Diversity, equity, and inclusion (DEI) are topics at staff, department, or team meetings.		
I model the priority of DEI in my staff or parent communications (emails, notes).		
School announcements feature DEI-related communications.		
Student voices on matters relating to DEI are heard.		
My colleagues understand that DEI is a priority and focus for me.		
Families at my school understand that DEI is a priority for our school community.		
We communicate in multiple languages in visuals and written documents.		
I/we use DEI-related questions as part of my/our hiring and interview process.		
Our vision/mission and goal statements include DEI as priorities.		
Family engagement at my school includes people with diverse perspectives and experiences.		
The professional development I lead or participate in includes DEI awareness, skills, and understanding.		
I support DEI goals for staff that are challenging but also attainable.		
I encourage other staff to set personal goals for their own DEI journey.		

REFLECTION QUESTIONS

What actions do you feel proud of?
What areas would you identify as needing growth?
What steps can you take to improve your leadership for equity?

References

Adams, et al. (2021). *Map: See which states have passed critical race theory bills.* NBC News. Retrieved from https://www.nbcnews.com/news/nbcblk/map-see -which-states-have-passed-critical-race-theory-bills-n1271215

Adichie, C. (2009). *The danger of a single story* [Video]. TEDGlobal Conferences. Retrieved from https://www.ted.com/talks/chimamanda_ngozi_adichie_the _danger_of_a_single_story/

Allen, J. (2021). *My voice is a trumpet.* New York: Flamingo Books.

American Association of School Librarians. (2022). *National School Library Standards.* Retrieved from https://standards.aasl.org/framework

American Psychological Association Mental Health Primers (2023). *Students exploring gender identity.* Retrieved from https://www.apa.org/ed/schools/ primer/gender-identity

Amick, E. [@emilyinyourphone]. (n.d.). Posts [Instagram profile]. Instagram. Retrieved April 30, 2023, from https://www.instagram.com/emilyinyourphone

Apple, M. W. (1971). The hidden curriculum and the nature of conflict. *Interchange, 2*(4), 27–40.

Bamberg, M., & Andrews, M. (2004). *Considering counter narratives: Narrating, resisting, making sense.* Amsterdam: John Benjamins.

Banks, J. A., & Banks, C. A. M. (Eds.). (2019). *Multicultural education: Issues and perspectives.* New York: Wiley.

Bishop, R. S. (1990, March). *Windows and mirrors: Children's books and parallel cultures* [Paper presentation], pp. 3–12. California State University Reading Conference, San Bernardino: 14th Annual Conference.

Bridges, R. (2022). *I am Ruby Bridges.* New York: Scholastic.

Brown, B. (2015). *Daring greatly: How the courage to be vulnerable transforms the way we live, love, parent, and lead.* New York: Avery.

Buchanan-Rivera, E. (2022). *Identity affirming classrooms: Spaces that center humanity*. London: Routledge.

Calkins, L. (2017). *A guide to the writing workshop: Intermediate grades*. Portsmouth, NH: Heinemann.

Campano, G. (2006). *Immigrant students and literacy: Reading, writing, and remembering*. New York: Teachers College Press.

Campano, G., Ghiso, M. P., & Welch, B. J. (2016). *Partnering with immigrant communities: Action through literacy*. New York: Teachers College Press.

Carroll, L. (1981). *Alice's adventures in wonderland and through the looking-glass*. New York: Bantam Classics.

Chang, E., & Gamez, R. (2022). Educational leadership as accompaniment: From managing to cultivating youth activism. *Teachers College Record, 124*(9), 65–90.

Choi, Y. (2003). *The name jar*. New York: Dragonfly Books.

Comber, B., Thomson, P., & Wells, M. (2001). Critical literacy finds a "place": Writing and social action in a low-income Australian grade 2/3 classroom. *Elementary School Journal, 101*(4), 451–464.

Costa, A., & Garmston, R. (2002). *Cognitive coaching: A foundation for renaissance schools*. Norwood, MA: Christopher-Gordon.

Costa, A., & Kallick, B. (2009). *Habits of mind across the curriculum*. Alexandria, VA: Association for Supervision and Curriculum Development.

Delpit, L. (2006). *Other people's children: Cultural conflict in the classroom*. New York: New Press.

Derting, K., & Johannes, S. (2020). *Cece loves science*. New York: Greenwillow Books.

Duckworth, A. (2018). *Grit: The power of passion and perseverance*. New York: Scribner.

Esteban-Guitart, M., & Moll, L. C. (2014). Funds of identity: A new concept based on the funds of knowledge approach. *Culture & Psychology, 20*(1), 31–48.

Freire, P. (1970). *Pedagogy of the oppressed*. London: Penguin.

Gee, J. P. (2000). Chapter 3: Identity as an analytic lens for research in education. *Review of Research in Education, 25*(1), 99–125.

Gee, J. P. (2005). *An introduction to discourse analysis*. New York: Routledge.

Genishi, C., & Dyson, A. H. (2009). *Children, language, and literacy: Diverse learners in diverse times*. New York: Teachers College Press.

Ghiso, M. P. (2016). The laundromat as the transnational local: Young children's literacies of interdependence. *Teachers College Record, 118*(1), 1–46.

Gorman, A. (2021). *Change sings: A children's anthem*. New York: Viking.

Hammond, Z. (2014). *Culturally responsive teaching and the brain: Promoting authentic engagement and rigor among culturally and linguistically diverse students*. Thousand Oaks, CA: Corwin.

Hannah-Jones, N., & Watson, R. (2021). *The 1619 Project: Born on the water*. New York: Penguin Random House.

Harari, Y. (2018). *Sapiens: A brief history of humankind*. Toronto, ON: McClelland & Stewart.

Ho, J. (2021). *Eyes that kiss in the corners*. New York: HarperCollins.

Hollins, C. (2023). *Inside out: The equity leader's guide to undoing institutional racism*. Gabriola Island, BC: New Society.

Hollins, C., & Govan, I. (2015). *Diversity, equity, and inclusion: Strategies for facilitating conversations on race.* Lanham, MD: Rowman & Littlefield.

Institute for the Habits of Mind (2022). Retrieved from https://www.habitsofmindinstitute.org

James, L. (2020). *I promise.* New York: HarperCollins.

Johns Hopkins University. (2023). *The power of positive thinking.* Retrieved from https://www.hopkinsmedicine.org/health/wellness-and-prevention/the-power-of-positive-thinking

Johnston, P. (2004). *Choice words.* Portland, ME: Stenhouse.

Jones, S. (2006). *Girls, social class, and literacy: What teachers can do to make a difference.* Portsmouth, NH: Heinemann.

Kay, M. (2018). *Not light, but fire: How to lead meaningful race conversations in the classroom.* Portsmouth, NH: Stenhouse.

Kendi, I. X. (2019). *How to be an antiracist.* London: One World.

King Jr., M. L. (2000). *Why we can't wait.* London: Penguin.

Kleinrock, L. (2021). *Start here, start now: A guide to antibias and antiracist work in your school community.* Portsmouth, NH: Heinemann.

Kriete, R., & Davis, C. (2014). *The morning meeting book.* Turners Falls, MA: Center for Responsive Schools.

Kunkel, A. (2020). *Digging for words: Jose Alberto Gutierrez and the library he built.* New York: Schwartz & Wade Books.

Kuypers, L. (2011). *Zones of regulation: A curriculum designed to foster self-regulation and emotional control.* San Jose, CA: Think Social.

Ladson-Billings, G. (1995). Toward a theory of culturally relevant pedagogy. *American Educational Research Journal, 32*(3), 465–491.

Ladson-Billings, G. (2009). *The dreamkeepers.* San Francisco: Jossey-Bass.

Ladson-Billings, G. (2014). Culturally relevant pedagogy 2.0: Aka the remix. *Harvard Educational Review, 84*(1), 74–84.

Lester, J. (2008). *Let's talk about race.* New York: HarperCollins.

Little, J. W., & Bartlett, L. (2010). The teacher workforce and problems of educational equity. *Review of Research in Education, 34*(1), 285–328.

Loyola Marymount University Implicit Bias Task Force. (2016). *Test your implicit bias—Implicit Association Test (IAT).* Retrieved from https://www.resources.lmu.edu/dei/initiativesprograms/implicitbiasinitiative/whatisimplicitbias/

Luttrell, W. (2013). Children's counter-narratives of care: Towards educational justice. *Children & Society, 27*(4), 295–308.

Lyon, G. E. (1999). *Where I'm from: Where poems are from.* Spring, TX: Absey.

Madison, M., Ralli, J., & Roxas, I. (2021). *Our skin: A first conversation about race.* New York: Rise.

Miller, D. (2008). *Teaching with intention: Defining beliefs, aligning practice, taking action.* Portland, ME: Stenhouse.

Morales, A. (2021). *Areli is a dreamer: A true story by Areli Morales, a DACA recipient.* New York: Random House.

Muhammad, G. (2020). *Cultivating genius: An equity framework for culturally and historically responsive literacy.* New York: Scholastic.

Munsch, R. (1980). *The paper bag princess.* Des Moines, IA: Turtleback Books.

National Center for Restorative Justice (2023). Seattle, WA. Retrieved from https://www.nationalcenterforrestorativejustice.com

National Governors Association. (2010). *Common Core State Standards.* Washington, DC: National Governors Association.

Paley, V. (1998). *The girl with the brown crayon: How children use stories to shape their lives.* Cambridge, MA: Harvard University Press.

Plachowski, T. J. (2019). Reflections of preservice teachers of color: Implications for the teacher demographic diversity gap. *Education Sciences, 9*(2), 144.

Ross, L. (2021). *Don't call people out—call them in* [Video]. TED talk. Retrieved from https://www.youtube.com/watch?v=xw_720iqdss

Sheth, S. (2018). *Always Anjali.* Cambridge, MA: Mango & Marigold.

Singleton, G. (2015). *Courageous conversations about race: A field guide for achieving equity in schools.* Thousand Oaks, CA: Corwin.

Southern Poverty Law Center (2021). *Frameworks.* Learning for Justice. Retrieved from https://www.learningforjustice.org/frameworks

Sparks, D. (2002, Fall). Conversations about race need to be fearless: A conversation with Glenn Singleton. *Journal of Staff Development, 23*(4). Retrieved from https://intranet.oprfhs.org/board-of-education/board_meetings/Special_Meetings/Packets/2007/020908.pdf

Steele, C. (2010). *Whistling Vivaldi: How stereotypes affect us and what we can do.* New York: Norton.

Suggs, E. (2019, December 29). Five things to know about Congressman John Lewis. *Atlanta Journal-Constitution.* Retrieved from https://www.ajc.com/news/five-things-know-about-congressman-john-lewis/uzHfUBLepoRaRnwvjlmpkK/

Thompkins-Bigelow, J. (2020). *Your name is a song.* Seattle, WA: Innovation.

Tilhou, R. C. (2020). The morning meeting: Fostering a participatory democracy begins with youth in public education. *Democracy & Education, 28*(2), 1–11. Retrieved from https://democracyeducationjournal.org/home/vol28/iss2/5/

Tough, P. (2013). *How children succeed: Grit, curiosity, and the hidden power of character.* Boston: Houghton Mifflin Harcourt.

Vagianos, A. (2015, June 2). *Ruth Bader Ginsburg tells young women: "Fight for the things you care about."* Harvard Radcliffe Institute. Retrieved from https://www.radcliffe.harvard.edu/news-and-ideas/ruth-bader-ginsburg-tells-young-women-fight-for-the-things-you-care-about

Vasquez, V. (2001). Constructing a critical curriculum with young children. In B. Comber & A. Simpson (Eds.), *Negotiating critical literacies in classrooms.* London: Routledge.

White, S. (2019). *Creating a learning environment where all kids feel valued.* Edutopia. Retrieved from https://www.edutopia.org/article/creating-learning-environment-where-all-kids-feel-valued

Williams, B. (2023). Institute Success [Quote]. Retrieved from https://institute-success.com/library/you-may-find-that-making-a-difference-for-others-makes-the-biggest-difference-in-you-brian-williams/

Woodson, J. (2001). *The other side.* New York: Penguin Random House.

Yellen, J. L. (2020, May). *The history of women's work and wages and how it has created success for us all.* The Brookings Institution. Retrieved from https://www.brookings.edu/essay/the-history-of-womens-work-and-wages-and-how-it

-has-created-success-for-us-all/#:~:text=Between%20the%201930s%20and%20
mid,factors%20contributed%20to%20this%20rise

Zacher, J. C. (2009). Christina's worlds: Negotiating childhood in the city. *Educational Studies, 45*(3), 262–279.

Zalaznik, M. (2021). *2 states, and counting, ban critical race theory in schools*. District Administration. Retrieved from https://districtadministration.com/states-ban -teaching-critical-race-theory-schools/

Zhang, K. (2022). *Amy Wu and the warm welcome*. New York: Simon & Schuster.

About the Authors

ALYSON LAMONT, EDD

Alyson Lamont is a district-level instructional specialist and has taught university courses, supervised student teachers, worked on grant-funded research projects, and consulted. Her areas of expertise include literacy, educational technology integration, and equity initiatives. She holds a doctor of education degree in curriculum and teaching from Teachers College, Columbia University. Alyson's scholarly work has been published in several academic journals: *Phi Delta Kappan, Contemporary Issues in Early Childhood, Berkeley Review of Education,* and the *English Record.* She presents at local and national conferences.

PAMELA WASHINGTON

Pamela Washington serves as an elementary principal where she provides instructional leadership for a staff of sixty. Previously Pamela was an assistant principal, dean of students, literacy coach, and elementary teacher. In her various roles, she has provided leadership in balanced literacy, data-driven decision-making, instructional practices, and diversity, equity, and inclusion. As an adjunct instructor for Seattle University, Pamela supervised and coached teachers in the Masters in Teaching Reading Endorsement Program. Pamela is a GLAD (Guided Language Acquisition Design) key trainer and has collaboratively developed district-wide curricula in the content areas of reading and writing.

EMILIE HARD

Emilie Hard was the assistant superintendent for teaching and learning in a large school district and served as the director of equity in another school district. Her former positions include elementary principal, curriculum developer, and classroom teacher. She earned her master's degree in curriculum and instruction and administrative credentials from the University of Oregon and supervised student teachers for Seattle University. She supports principal interns through the University of Washington, has coauthored numerous Reader's Workshop units for school districts, and was a contributing author to *Activating and Engaging Habits of Mind* (Costa & Kallick, 2000), *Habits of Mind across the Curriculum* (Costa & Kallick, 2009), and *Learning and Leading with Habits of Mind* (Costa & Kallick, 2008).